TRIUMPH
—— OVER ——
Failure and Fear

Finding Your Resilience in the Face of Adversity

SALLY ALLEN

HUGO HOUSE PUBLISHERS, LTD.

Triumph Over Failure and Fear: Finding Your Resilience in the Face of Adversity

©2021 Sally Allen. All rights reserved. No part of this publication may be reproduced or transmitted in any form or by any means, mechanical or electronic, including photocopying and recording, or by any information storage and retrieval system, without permission in writing from the author or publisher (except by a reviewer, who may quote brief passages and/or short brief video clips in a review).

ISBN: 978-1-948261-42-5

Library of Congress Control Number: 2021909287

Cover design & interior layout: Ronda Taylor, HeartWorkCreative.com

Hugo House Publishers, Ltd.
Austin, TX • Denver, CO
www.HugoHousePublishers.com

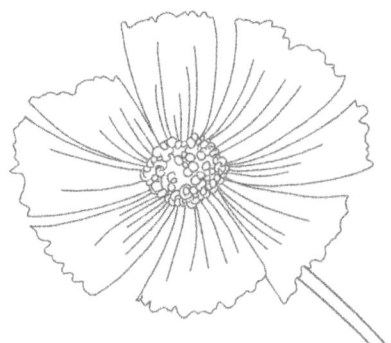

Dedication

To my faithfully charming and supportive husband and son. Be resilient.

And Mimi, I miss you every day!

Contents

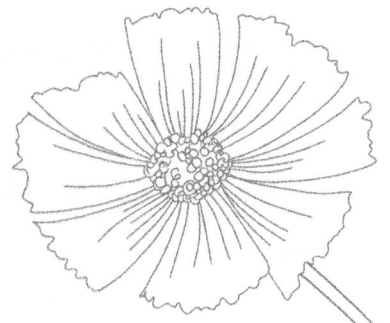

On My Beautiful Country. vii

Foreword ix

1. The Rain 1
2. Fifty Pills and a Missionary 9
3. Cinderella 21
4. The Arranged Marriage 33
5. Coming to America. 47
6. The Great Escape 57
7. The Train 75

| 8 | Take Back Your Power | . . . . 83 |

Acknowledgments 93

About the Author 95

Contact the Author 97

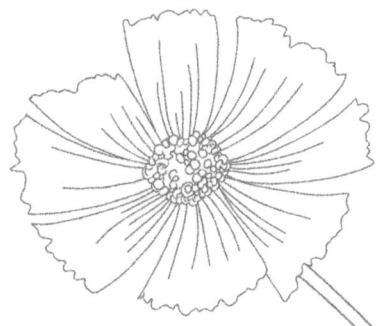

On My Beautiful Country

My story took place twenty-eight years ago in Guyana, located in South America. Guyana was and still is considered a third-world country.

Living a life of Resiliency in a third-world country is not easy, especially during my era. However, a lot has changed since then.

There is electricity, more roads, many more vehicles, and women drivers. Women are attending gyms without shame. Women are entrepreneurs and are empowered. Guyana is changing and trending upwards. It is a beautiful country with rich cultures and traditions.

I am proud of my country.

This is my story seen through my eyes and my recollection.

Foreword

In our lives, we are surrounded by so much wonder, beauty, and goodness: the magnificence of the natural world, human endeavors for broad social justice, individual selfless acts for the greater good, philanthropists who donate vast wealth for causes of decency and charity. These are but a few examples of the goodness that surrounds us. Further, if we are lucky within our personal experiences, we observe and hopefully participate in acts of goodwill, kindness, love, and compassion each day. Yet, in juxtaposition to this world of goodness is a world of sadness, brutality, and evil in which the weak and less fortunate are victims to those with the slightest edge in power, wealth, and social standing.

To a large extent, the relative levels of goodness versus evilness that we are exposed to, particularly at a young age, is determined by the greatest of all lotteries—the birth lottery. Each of us is given a single ticket that dictates where and when we are born, who our parents are, our birth order, and our gender.

Like so many of us from first-world countries, my own lottery ticket was pretty darn good. Born a white male, the youngest of three children in a middle-class family with a loving and nurturing mother, I lived in the US in a time of relative peace. All these things provided me and others with lottery picks like mine a stable nurturing environment protected from the evil side of our world until I was strong enough to understand and deal with such matters. Yet in my daily life, like most folks with good lottery tickets, I spend a good deal of time focusing and lamenting on the problems and issues in my life while I tend to forget just how fortunate my lottery pick was … that is until I read Sally's story.

Sally's ticket was, in a word, abysmal. Born into poverty in a third- world country, rejected, victimized, and brutalized by people that should have kept her safe, her painful saga continued through her twenties. Her young life was devoid of that safe, nurturing environment that those with good lottery draws enjoyed. Yet, through courage, resolve, and resilience she was able to rise out of a tormented existence to lead a happy, full, and fulfilling life.

For someone who has known Sally as a good friend and colleague for years and never known any of this, the story of her young life is overwhelmingly sad, horrific, even shocking, but above all it is inspirational. In the broadest sense, it brings hope that the billions of other people born into similar circumstances can also find fulfilling lives full of love, compassion, and happiness just as Sally did. On a very personal level, Sally's story and the methods she employed to overcome the adver-

Foreword

sities in her life, are great tools for all of us (regardless of our lottery draw) to use to overcome challenges in our daily lives.

Thank you Sally for showing us a life well and truly lived. It is up to us to follow your shining example.

Rich Schneider
Las Vegas
March, 2021

1

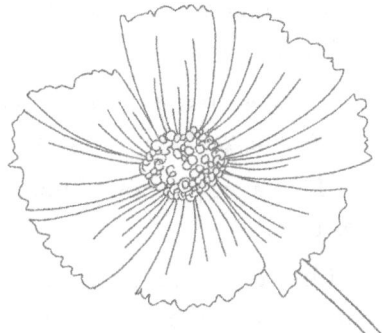

The Rain

"Courage is not the absence of fear, but rather the assessment that something else is more important than fear."

—FRANKLIN D. ROOSEVELT

I DID NOT KNOW THAT MY FIRST DAY OF KINDERGARTEN would be the day I grew up. My mother had dropped me off, but she forgot to pick me up. By the time I found my way home at the end of the day, I was no longer an innocent child who lacked awareness of my sad little world around me.

As I walked through this trauma on the way home, it felt like my soul was broken and lost. At six years old, I did not know how to cope or harness hope through the situation. I most definitely did not see any light at the end of any tunnel. As I sit here writing this, I have no idea how I survived that day.

As I got dressed in my precious little uniform for school that Monday, I felt like crying.

"I am a big girl now," I told myself. "I cannot cry; big girls don't cry."

I heard my mother calling my name. I got my backpack and ran down the stairs to meet her. It was cloudy and almost 100% humidity, as it always is in Guyana. Before we hit the gate to leave the house, I was already drenched with sweat, but I felt happy as I held my mom's hand and walked down the street to my school.

I did not know where my school was located, but I remembered crossing a bridge. It was an old wooden bridge that had been there for decades. As we crossed that bridge, I felt a little scared. I could not swim. I had this fleeting thought of falling into the water below and drowning. Little did I know, it was a premonition of what was to come.

Once I got to school, all nervousness flew out the window. Everyone, including my teacher, realized that I was an extrovert and could talk up a storm. While I scored points for being a chatterbox, it didn't hide the fact that I could not write the number three. I distinctly remembered my teacher making me trace it over and over on the blackboard.

As I traced for what seemed like the one-hundredth time, it began to rain. Sheets of water poured down, hammering against the thin metal roof. The rain sounded furious as it battered against the roof. Some of the children started crying,

1 • The Rain

causing a ripple effect. Before long, all of us were crying. Our teachers did their best to calm us down.

It was alarming as it rained and rained with no signs of stopping. However, the rain did not stop the day from moving on. Soon it was dismissal time. One-by-one all the kids left, and I was the only one there waiting for someone to get me. My teacher walked me out the door, locked it, and assured me someone was coming to pick me up.

That was forty years ago, and in my culture at the time, it was normal for kids that young to walk home by themselves. There were no school buses in my country. Since it was only my first day, I knew my mom would come back. Surely she would, I thought, because I made her promise over and over to pick me up. It seemed like I waited for hours. I couldn't tell how long, but I realized no one was coming to get me and I was on my own.

It continued to rain and started to get dark. It dawned on me that it would not stop raining, no matter how much I wished for that to happen. Finally, I mustered all my courage and ran out into the rain. As the torrents of water hit my head, I gasped. I didn't realize it was cold. I tucked my hands under my shirt, determined to get home. I looked around for landmarks as I ran down the street. Ah! There it was. The bridge we had crossed on our way to school. It was my saving grace, the light at the end of the tunnel—or so I thought. Little did I know what horror awaited me. Perhaps if I did, I would have stayed under that awning at school. However, I wouldn't give up that moment for the world. I am glad I experienced it. That moment opened my eyes and molded me into the person that I am today.

As I approached the bridge, it did not look the same. Panic rose from my stomach into my throat. I came to a screeching halt and stared in horror at the sight before me. One of the planks was missing from the bridge, and the water was raging through the gaping hole. My heart was racing so hard I felt like it would jump out of my chest. Then I heard screaming. I looked around, wondering who else was there. I realized it was me.

I stood there staring at the bridge for what seemed like an eternity. All I could think about was the bridge looked like a huge gap-toothed troll waiting to gobble me up. I continued to scream, hoping someone would come to my rescue. No one did. Looking back now, I felt not only terrified, but ashamed and abandoned. Why did my mom not want to come back for me? My six-year-old mind was too young to comprehend anything else beyond that.

However, even as a child, I was tenacious and was determined to get across that bridge. After I got my screaming under control, I walked slowly to the edge of the bridge. As I got closer, I realized it was slippery, and I quickly got down on my belly. I gasped as I sank into the cold mud, and I began to crawl. As I neared the gaping hole, I froze in fear and started to cry. "Will I ever make it home?" I thought. I sobbed louder, inching my way to the gap, feeling sorry for myself the entire time.

It seemed like hours had passed as I continued to inch my way closer to the wide opening. I had a job to do and focused intensely on the task at hand. But the hole seemed to get wider the closer I got to it. I grabbed onto the stable planks for dear life. Somewhere along the way, I stopped crying and felt confident. I can do this, I thought, as I inched my way closer and closer.

I finally got to the last plank before the opening. The water seemed like it was determined to carry away everything in its paths. I started shivering violently. I could turn back but, where would I go? Besides, the bridge was so slippery; I dared not stand up. I lay on my belly, eyeing the other side, wishing I could miraculously be there.

Without thinking, I closed my eyes and launched my body over the opening. As soon as my body propelled forward, I realized I had miscalculated the distance between the two sides. Naturally, the lower half of my tiny body hit the water. The current was strong, and I was sure it was going to drag me along with it. I started screaming again.

Thunder roared above as if it did not want to miss out on the madness below. Lightning bolts flashed across the sky like angry fire branding the heavens and punishing me for a crime I did not commit. The river continued to rage like a hungry lion. I screamed louder and louder as I clawed my way up out of the water. Not knowing or understanding where I got the strength, I catapulted to the other side of the bridge, rolled a few feet, and stopped. I sprawled out in the mud gasping for breath.

Finally, I was able to drag myself to the embankment. As my feet hit the edge, I fell and spiraled down, sucking in mud and my breath knocked out of me. As I struggled to breathe, the thunder and lightning continued to rage on, but instead of being afraid, I took it as encouragement. This time, it sounded like "Way to go. You did it." It was the only encouragement I would have for a long time. It was still raining when I finally got up and began to walk home. I looked around and sobbed quietly, realizing this had always been my life … and this was how it was going to be. The river, the rain, the thunder, the lightning—all were a poetic prophecy of what was ahead for my future.

PRESENT MOMENT

The bridge turned out to be a light at the end of the tunnel. It tested me—my strength, my resolve, and yes, my resilience—but I got through it. Later in life, I realized I was the one who was creating that light, as I had no support or safe space. That moment where I had to get over that bridge or die—literally—changed me forever.

We choose whether to create and harness light or whether we live in darkness. We *can* be healed and be restored from our broken past, but it is an intentional choice that we have to make.

Think back to your first childhood memory. Was it pleasant? Was it painful? Think about writing it down. You know the saying … don't let your past define you? I find that saying to be so untrue. Our past plays a part in who we are as adults, but we get to determine what role it plays. Know that no matter whether those memories are happy, sad, or traumatizing, *You* have a choice on how they define you, and that's the critical point.

When the realization hit me that I was alone and that my life basically sucked, I decided that I did not need anyone to take care of me. I was only six years old, but it did not matter. I did not know what I was doing at the time, but my decision to fend for myself has manifested itself repeatedly throughout my life. It helped me understand why I am driven to be independent and bold.

1 • The Rain

You see, after the bridge incident, I made a promise to myself that I would take care of my mother. I didn't need anyone to take care of me. I chose to stay in denial about why she did not pick me up that day from school, but in the back of my mind, I knew she didn't come to get me that day because she was drinking. That day I realized that my mom was an alcoholic, and from that day on, I followed her everywhere. As soon as I got home from school, I would hit up the bar where I knew she would be, and I would sit there with her until it was time to go home. I followed her around and took care of her until the morning she passed away in my arms.

Now let's not forget my fear of water back then. You see, up until a few years ago, I was still terrified of drowning. One day, I decided to change that. I refused to live in fear. Oddly enough, I love the ocean despite my near-death experience on the bridge. Go figure.

I am tenacious and determined even more than I was at six years old. I was going to learn how to swim. I signed up for swim lessons at Water Wings. What I did not know was that Water Wings is predominately for young children. As I walked into the facility on my first day, I almost died of humiliation and shame as I watched the young kids frolic in the water and swimming like fish. I was the only adult there.

I turned around and raced back to my car, defeated. I kept telling myself, I could never swim like those little kids. I was not going to humiliate myself. As I grabbed the car door handle, I thought to myself, cut the crap, Sally. You are not this frail six-year-old little girl trying to get across a raging river on an unstable bridge. Besides, you weren't wimpy back then. Now you are a grown woman and stronger. Turn around, suck it up, and go learn how to swim.

I walked back towards the facility with steely resolve. I was starting to feel confident again—then I met my swim coach. She was half my age. I lost all confidence as she demonstrated all the different strokes and breathing techniques. I stood there biting my lips, wishing I could just disappear.

As we got in the water, she showed me some more strokes and how to tread water. I was starting to enjoy it as I gained confidence. Then I tried to float; I immediately sank and sucked in a lung full of water. As I coughed it up, I realized it was salty. I inquired why. Come to find out, some kids had vomited in the pool that day, and they used salt to clean and sanitize the pool.

I couldn't believe it. What the heck? Vomit? Who knew that vomit could motivate me! I learned how to swim, float, and tread water that day, and I never went back ... and that's resilience, Friends, making hard choices and living through the consequences.

Listen, life is tough. Sometimes it takes swallowing someone else's "vomit" to galvanize us into action. Every time I read that sentence, I laugh out loud, but in a sense, it is true, isn't it?

Today, I scuba dive, snorkel and have no fear of water.

I'm also no longer afraid of finding out what's on the other side of the bridge.

2

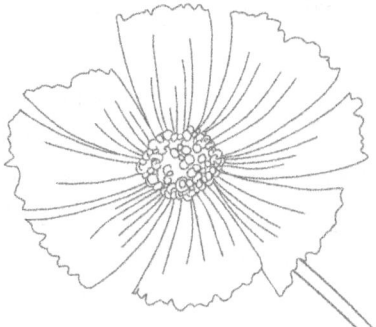

Fifty Pills and a Missionary

> *"Tragedy should be utilized as a source of strength. No matter what sort of difficulties, how painful the experience is, if we lose our hope, that's our real disaster."*
>
> —DALAI LAMA

WITHOUT HOPE, OUR MIND, BODY, AND SOUL LIVE IN A state of despair.

I started to understand the meaning of hope and hopelessness when I was eight years old. My hope came through a supernatural source, God. He was not done with my story, so He intervened and provided me with a resource that literally saved my life. He gave me hope and helped me to become the person I am today.

You see, I was desperate for my story to end. After the bridge incident, my entire life was magnified before my eyes. Before that incident, I was oblivious and had no idea of how neglected I was. After that incident, my eyes were open to the abandonment and lack of love in my life. I felt desperate and lost, and by the time I was eight years old, I felt like I was done with life. I had no desire to live.

My father passed away when I was two years old. My mother and I lived with my Uncle Sanjay and Aunt Sheela, and their two children, Naya and Kumar. Since my mom never cooked or took care of me, she constantly sent me off to the neighbors to be fed. Sheela and her family refused to offer anything to us. We lived in a small village and everyone knew everyone's business, so our neighbors had no issues providing food to me. I should mention I had nine other siblings, whom I barely knew because they were grown and had left home.

As I got older, I started to understand that my mom had tried several times to abort me, but I was the fetus that never quit. I continued to follow mom around and took care of her. I remember learning how to trick her into going home and going to bed. I made up stuff like, "I bet you cannot walk home right now." She was all too happy to show me she could walk home. Then I would say, "I bet you cannot go up the stairs." She, of course, had to show me she was sober enough to walk up the stairs—my first exposure to and experience with alcoholics.

I recently reflected on those moments. They are sad and still painful. I realize my mom did not have anyone to take care of her, and she did not know how to take care of herself. I also realized she had her demons that she was struggling with. Only someone with some severe issues would strangle a child and demand that the child profess love for them.

This abuse started when I was seven years old. I woke up one night with her fingers around my throat. I kicked and fought to try to pry her fingers away from my throat. She stopped and looked at me, her eyes glazed over.

"Do you love me?" She whispered. I nodded my head, afraid to speak.

As I sit here writing this, tears streaming down my face, I feel extreme sadness. What were her demons? I do not and cannot pretend to understand. What I do know is that I wish I knew back then how to help her. I wish I knew what to do. It never occurred to me to share what was going on with anyone, or perhaps deep down inside, I knew that no one would care.

Sanjay and his family lived their own life. They had their demons they were battling. Sanjay was also an alcoholic and would physically abuse Sheela. Sheela, on the other hand, despised our family. I have met two very evil people in my life; she was one of them. She hated that my mother and I were living with them. She did not disguise that she detested us. I steered clear of her and her family.

Sanjay's family was dysfunctional, but it also made me realize what I was missing in life. Sheela would cook and feed her children while I locked myself in my room, starving. I never understood how one human could treat another human being that way. As I sat in my room while their family was having dinner, I would pretend I had lots of money to feed the poor and needy. I made a promise to myself that one day I would help the needy and poor. Even then, in my misery, I started building my resiliency.

One day, I overheard Sheela and our neighbors talking about someone who had taken pills and died. I asked what died meant, and Sheela told me that the person went to sleep forever. What a great idea! I was only at peace when I was asleep. Wouldn't it be great if I never had to wake up? The more I thought about the idea, the more excited I got. I was tired of chasing my mom from bar to bar. I was tired of not having food to eat. I was tired of being abused by my mom night after night. I was tired of the violence I witnessed in our house when Sanjay would physically abuse Sheela. Most of all, I was tired of Sheela causing strife in our family.

Sheela would make up stories about something that my mom did to her, and Sanjay would take it out on mom. I do not have the courage or guts to go into details about that abuse. It is still horrifying. I remember hiding under my bed, my heart pounding when the abuse was taking place. I felt hopeless, helpless, and angry because I could not do anything about it. I felt this person clawing inside of me to jump out and do something, but I repressed her. What could I do? I was just a little girl, and I knew I would get a good beating if I intervened.

As I sit writing this, my heart is aching, and I feel overwhelming sadness. I cannot stop crying. Not only am I crying for that little girl who hid under the bed, but I cry for the little girls today who still do not have a voice. I cry for those girls who have grown up and live that vicious cycle repeatedly. I hope my words make their way to you and help you seek and find the deliverance we all need.

2 • Fifty Pills and a Missionary

I often wonder if my mother ever forgave me for not intervening. I have forgiven that little girl. I look at her with compassion and love. She survived, and I still sometimes wonder how she did and how she became the person she is today.

So now you know why going to sleep forever sounded so wonderful to me. I pondered about that for days, wondering if I dared to do it. Then fate intervened. One bright Saturday morning, I was cleaning my room when I found a bottle filled with pills. Could this be real? It was too good to be true.

I sat there trembling in anticipation and excitement and a tinge of sadness as I clutched the bottle full of pills. I had no idea to this day what type of drugs they were, but all I could think about was going to sleep forever. I was about to be saved. I shook the bottle; it felt full. My heart raced as I opened it. No one was home. I could do this, and no one would know, I thought. The relief I felt about never having to wake up to the nightmare of my life was so palpable. I just knew in my heart that it was the right thing to do.

Sitting here thinking about this story, I paused to think about my son, Richard. He is now twenty-six years old. I cannot imagine Richard trying to take his life because it was so horrific. I would die in a heartbeat for my son. I am so thankful I was able to break that vicious cycle.

I imagine my tiny, eight-year-old self, sitting on the bed contemplating going to sleep forever, and my heart is breaking over and over again. My solace is that going through all that trauma and drama made me the person I am today.

I got up from the bed and slowly walked to the kitchen. Funny, it was a lovely sunny day. All the house windows were open, and I could feel the humid breeze gently floating through the house as I filled a glass with water. I went back to my room and closed my two windows and sat on the bed. I could feel the thin mattress sagging under me. I thought to myself, "How come I never noticed this before?" I realized I was procrastinating. I was scared, but my desire to put out my light and be in darkness forever was stronger.

I grabbed the glass of water and popped the cap of the pill bottle. I poured all the pills on the bed. I gingerly picked up one and popped it in my mouth. I waited a minute, nothing happened. Then I popped two, three, four, five, yet I felt nothing. I continued to wash down the pills. I didn't stop until I had swallowed 50 pills. Suddenly the room started spinning. I quickly grabbed a pillow, lay down, and stared up at the ceiling. "I feel at peace." I smiled as I closed my eyes and passed out.

I must have slept all day because when I woke up, it was almost dark. I felt nauseous and I was drenched in sweat. I started convulsing and couldn't stop. My eyes swam around the room. The pink walls seem to be closing in on me. They zoomed in and out. I tried to scream, but no sound came out of my mouth. What was happening to me? Then it hit me; I had taken pills to go to sleep. I jack-knifed into a sitting position, but pain stabbed behind my eyes. I fell back on the pillow and passed out again. My last thought was, "Why am I awake? I'm supposed to be sleeping forever." If you are tracking with me, you will not be surprised that no one came to seek me out or find out if I was okay. My mother was out drinking.

When I woke up again, I could not move, but I heard my mother snoring gently beside me. Did she know what I did? Would she care? I tried to swat the bugs crawling under my skin. I quickly realized there were no bugs. How can they be under my skin? I started rubbing my arms feverishly. I got out of bed and turned on the kerosene lamp and started shaking in horror as I looked up at the ceiling. What was that on the ceiling? Gargoyles?

I did not know it at the time, but I was hallucinating. There were hundreds of tiny creatures on the ceiling. They looked like large multicolored dragons. I tried to scream, but no sounds came out of my mouth. I crawled to the corner of the room and sat there, hugging my knees close to my chest. I prayed for the dragons to go away. I kept telling myself that it was not happening. Maybe this is sleeping forever? I grew up in a Muslim home and believed in hell. Perhaps I was in hell. Are dragons real in hell? To say I was scared out of my mind is an understatement. I started to convulse violently again as I passed out on the floor.

The next morning, I woke up still sitting against the wall. I tried to stand up and started to retch. There was nothing in my stomach, and I dry heaved for what seemed like an eternity. My ribs felt like they were popping off. I looked around for my mother. I wanted to tell her what I had done. Maybe I needed to see a doctor. Mom was gone.

I changed my clothes and gingerly crept out of my room to tell someone what I had done. I heard Sheela washing clothes downstairs. The sound of the washing paddle felt like a jackhammer against my head. She took one look at me and stopped what she was doing.

"What did you do now?" She asked.

I told her what I did. She looked around and cocked her head as if she was in deep thought. Then she said, "You must not tell anyone about this, or you will get into trouble for taking all those pills."

Somehow, I knew that was the wrong thing to say, but at the time, I could not wrap my brain around why it was wrong. Years later, as I recalled that story, I realized she scared me into not telling anyone because she hoped for me to die. I often wonder why she hated my mother and me so much. You see, darkness does not like light, and God had plans for me. Nothing was going to stop those plans, not even Sheela.

Did I mention that I was tenacious? I was determined to go to sleep forever. I devised a plan to try the following Saturday again. I was up early and went pill hunting. I found two more bottles of pills. I got a glass of water and sat down on the bed, contemplating how many pills would do the trick this time. I was still exhausted from being sick from the last set of drugs. I wondered if I would get the desired result this time if I took more. What would be the correct dosage, I wondered? Maybe sixty? I closed my eyes and started counting.

I laid all the pills out on the bed, grabbed two and brought them to my mouth when I heard a voice coming from outside. "Hello, is anyone home?"

I paused. "Who dares to interrupt me?" I thought.

I crawled to my window and peeked down. I could not see the person. So I slid off the bed and slowly walked down the stairs. I was still tired and weak. Every step took tremendous effort. I was shaking by the time I got to the gate. As I approached the gate, I stopped dead in my tracks. I felt my jaw literally drop. Did I mention? We are dark-skinned and short in stature in my country. My ancestors are from India and Pakistan, and I had never seen a Caucasian person in my life. He stood at six feet tall; light skin and curly blonde hair seemed to gleam in the sun. He was wearing a loose red shirt and white slacks, and his sparkling green eyes twinkled as he beckoned me to come closer. I felt my heart racing. Who is this? What does he want?

"I have a gift for you," he almost whispered.

A gift? No one had ever given me a gift before. I slowly made my way to the gate. As I approached, his face changed into one of concern.

"Are you okay?" he asked. His voice was like music to my ears. Did he just ask if I was okay?

I shook my head, afraid to speak. His concern brought a lump to my throat. He reached into his bag and pulled out a small red book. The spine was gold, and the words outside were gold. I was too far away to read the words. I inched closer to the gate and looked at his white fingers wrapped around the book. I was fascinated by the beautiful gift but even more intrigued about why he was giving it to me. What was the catch?

I reached out and touched the book. He opened his fingers and held the book in the palm of his hand. I stepped back as he stretched out his arm to give it to me. Without giving it more of a thought, I reached out, still an arm's length away, and quickly snatched it from his palm.

I looked up, and he was smiling. I can still picture that smile. It was kind but was filled with concern.

"Do you know who Jesus is?" He asked. I shook my head.

Then he said, "Jesus loves you," and walked away.

I have never heard about Jesus. I clutched the book to my chest. I did not know how to react; maybe I should thank the stranger. I turned around to thank him, but he was gone. Just a few months earlier, on November 27, I proudly told my teacher it was my birthday. She looked at me sadly and said to me that my birthday had passed. It was November 22. I was too young to feel shame and embarrassment, but I did feel sadness. I knew that Sheela celebrated Naya's and Kumar's birthdays. I understood then that no one ever remembered my birthday, not even my mother. There was a slim chance for a gift!

As I walked to my bedroom (Notice that pattern? I spent most of my childhood in the bedroom), I read the words *New Tes-ta-ment* on the front of the cover. "What does that mean?" I had no idea. I started flipping through the pages. I only owned two novels, but I had read them repeatedly, and was ready for something new as I loved to read.

This book was different. It had words I did not understand. I kept thumbing through it, hoping to find something that would help me comprehend. As I was flipping through, I found a passage that told the story of Jesus walking on water. I read it repeatedly. I was fascinated by this dude who walked on water. Didn't the blonde-haired man mention that Jesus loves me?

I spent all day reading and re-reading that book. Who are you? Why do you love me? How can you walk on water? I got no answer, but in my eight-year-old mind, it was awesome having someone to talk to who loved me. I pictured Jesus with flaming red hair and piercing blue eyes sitting beside me and listening to me pour my heart out. I told him everything about me. I just talked and talked and talked until I passed out again. When I woke up that day, I felt purged and cleaned. That day I got my imaginary friend. The daily unloading to my imaginary friend helped me so much that, after a week, I forgot about wanting to go to sleep forever.

I made promises to Him that I would never treat people the way I was being treated. I would only love and care for people. I promised I would never have kids either. In my eight-year-old mind, moms were all mean and abusive. Thankfully, that turned out to not be accurate. At that point, without realizing it, I had started to shift my mindset. I had begun to write my own story.

PRESENT MOMENT

This is not religious book, but I hope you understand that hope comes in all forms. This is how my hope came: through my Savior. His love became my saving grace. As you continue to read, you will see how I overcame various obstacles. I relied more and more on my ability and my imaginary friend to be resilient.

You see, determination coupled with hope are powerful tools, but what happens when the initial adrenaline wears off? What keeps us going? What is our solid ground?

I will tell you my little secret; I found my solid ground is built on courage and faith. These two qualities are unshakable in me. They are my foundations of resilience. They don't change, even when everything else changes around me. They remain my constant.

Courage right now is me writing this at 2 a.m., pouring my heart and soul into my fingers as I pound the keyboard. At the beginning of this chapter, I was terrified because writing about myself is one of the hardest things I have done. However, by the end of this chapter, I had faith. You see, I knew if I could finish this chapter, I could finish this book.

I wish you the same kind of courage, hope, and determination to see the hard things through. This kind of foundation can spur you into action. Part of resilience is being able to take back your life and write your story. When I say, "Write your story," I mean take control of your life, be the person that orchestrates your life. For so long, everyone dictated my life; at one point, I had no identity. I needed to figure out who I was to take my life back and make my own decisions. Once I started making my own decisions, it was as if a bird were set free. I had my own two wings. I could fly. That's what I want for you to find in yourself. All it takes is you digging deep and finding what is worth fighting for.

It doesn't matter if you have a real friend, an imaginary friend, an advocate, or a mentor. Take your pick. Resilience comes when you find your values and foundations and have someone who can assist you in your journey. Mine helped me find courage and faith. With those firmly in place, I had hope—and do still to this day.

Sometimes that is all we need.

3

Cinderella

"We are only as sick as our secrets."

—STEPHEN KING

Life continued chugging along. Thank goodness I had found my imaginary friend. He was the catalyst that propelled me to keep moving forward. My imaginary friend was not only all I had, but everything I needed.

My mom was sick and I needed help. My aunt and uncle did nothing.

I did my best to care for her. I made soup and tried to feed her, but she spat it up and refused to eat. I was twelve years old when she died. I distinctly remember that event as if it were yesterday.

She had been in bed for three days very ill. I remembered Sanjay asking me if she was inebriated. It was common for her to be in an intoxicated condition for days at a time. No she was not drunk. I tried to convince my uncle that mom was ill, but he did not believe me. I cringe with embarrassment as I write this—I felt relieved she was not out and about drinking or abusing me. If not getting intoxicated meant that I had to take care of her, then I would.

It was night three of taking care of mom. I had fallen asleep exhausted. I woke up in a daze as I felt her shaking my shoulders. I sat up, leaned against the wall, and held her in my arms. I figured she had a bad dream. God knows I have had enough of those. As I dozed off, I heard the horn at the sugar estate go off twelve times. It was midnight. I fell asleep in the sitting position, holding my mom tightly in my arms.

It was daylight when I woke up. My mom's head was still in my lap. She had not moved. Her face was turned away from me, and so I could not see it. She felt heavier than when she originally fell asleep on my lap. I was sore, and my legs were numb, but I was afraid to move because I did not want to wake her up. I sat there contemplating what to do. Finally, I touched her face to wake her up. I thought it was odd that her face was icy cold. I turned her head face up and froze in horror. Her eyes were opened wide, her jaw was slack, and white foam caked around her mouth. I felt all the air sucked out of my body. I tried to scream, but no sound came out.

I tried to drag myself out from under my mom's dead weight. In my haste to get out, my feet got caught in the sheets. I slipped and fell, hitting my head on the side of the bed. I lay on the floor, stunned. Did my mom pass away in my arms? Was

3 • Cinderella

I cradling her dead body all night? Right about then, I found my voice and started screaming. Sanjay was home that day. He rushed into the room to see what the commotion was about.

I often pondered that day, trying to understand why I was screaming and scurrying away from my mom's body. My family and culture were so ingrained with superstition and folklore that I was terrified of the dead. I was convinced that because she died in my arms and I held her lifeless body through the night, her ghost would never leave me. It would always be attached to me. It's a weird superstition as a child that followed me far into adulthood. I no longer feel that way, but sometimes the ghosts of our past never really leave us, do they?

Sheela was very sympathetic on that day. She told me I did not have to do any of my chores. I remember thinking that my reprieve was "just for today." Tomorrow, things would go back to normal. I learned that day not to get too comfortable or complacent in a momentary lull. Things would change. For the longest while, I did not know how to live in the moment. It took me years and lots of practice to love and live in the moment. Life is too short not to enjoy those serendipity instances and learn from the inconvenient ones. Today I love every minute of my life: the good, the bad, and the ugly.

Later that fateful morning, Sanjay and my two other neighbors brought in an icebox and placed my mom in it. She was going to be buried the next day. Autopsies are not a big priority in my country, especially in the Muslim tradition. For religious reasons, they do not cut open the bodies. It's considered a violation of the body. Everyone seems to agree that mom died of a heart attack.

Mom was kept in the icebox in the middle of the living room. I had to pass it every time I went to the bedroom. I was genuinely traumatized by the icebox sitting there. To this day, I am still uncomfortable at funerals with open caskets. Don't laugh, but whenever I attend an open-casket funeral, I stay by the door in case I need to run. I am not sure why I would need to run. It is almost comical. We do bring a lot of our past into the future. There is so much tradition and culture ingrained in us from our past, we choose whether they haunt us. Since I do not attend many funerals with open caskets, I let this one "haunt" me. Ha!

On the day of my mom's funeral, the body was bathed and dressed in the living room. I sat in my room filled with mixed emotions. I can still hear the sound of the sloshing buckets of water as she was prepared for the funeral. After she was placed in the coffin, I came out of the room but walked back to the room and started crying. I realized now that I was crying because she looked peaceful. I had only seen her look peaceful once or twice in all my twelve years with her. I felt relieved for her. She was finally at rest, no longer tormented by her demons. Then I cried for me, knowing what lay ahead of me living with Sheela and her family.

It was an open-coffin funeral. Everyone came from our village. As they huddled around the coffin, everyone made sure I was at the very head of it. I was terrified and shaking, trying to be brave. I wanted to be as far away as possible. I heard many whispers…. "Poor child, what is she going to do now?" "Bless Sanjay and Sheela for taking care of her." "This child loved her momma." "This child is in shock." "She did not

3 • Cinderella

shed a tear." On and on it went for hours: the endless hugs and kisses. I was exhausted.

Finally, the coffin was taken away, and I breathed a sigh of relief. Just like that, my mom was gone. I went back to my room, grabbed one of her dresses, sank to the floor, and sobbed. Now I was really alone. I grabbed my red New Testament from under my pillow, which was now tattered and torn, and I held it close to my chest. I remembered whispering, "Now it's just you and me, Friend."

Three days after my mom's funeral, Sheela lay down the ground rules. I was to cook, clean, scrub the outhouse, clean the yard daily, and perform many more chores. I was not surprised; I knew it was coming. I began my new routine. Every day I would wake up, go to school, come home, cook, clean, wash up, do my homework, and head to my room. My room was my only safe space. It was the routine until one day when I realized there was an unwritten rule.

I had cooked dinner that day and was very hungry. I usually did not eat with the family. I would wait until they were all done eating before I ate. That day, since I was famished, I decided to eat right after I was done cooking. As I walked over to the table, Sheela caught me. She took my plate and walked back to the kitchen. I stood at the table, trying to figure out what just happened. Then I realized, as long as I was eating leftovers, I could eat. Otherwise, I could not eat. It was a not-too-subtle way of letting me know my place in their lives. I learned a valuable lesson that day. I also pledged to myself that I would never treat anyone that way.

As I think about my uncle and his family, I grieve for them and feel a sense of deep sadness and regret. I wish things could be better. I tried to reconcile with them a few years ago but to no avail. Some kinds of "toxic" are like grease fires; we cannot put them out. I fantasized that Naya and I would be like sisters, thick as thieves, but that was never the case.

Through daily cleaning of our yard, I found that I loved plants. My favorites were the marigold flowers. My neighbor gave me some seeds, and I felt much joy planting them. I spent hours toiling and watering. That soothed my soul and brought me peace. One day, Naya wanted me to play with her. I was not interested. By now, you have probably figured out this much; I did not play much as a child. I was more interested in reading my New Testament and finding peace. However, Naya did not take my rejection to play well. She ran to the yard screaming, "I am going to get you for this!"

The next thing I knew, she got down on her hands and knees and tore up all the marigold flowers that were just blooming. I stared in disbelief as she tore up all the flowers. Her face was contorted and red as she furiously attacked the plants. I felt anger welling up inside of me. I ran over to her and grabbed her arms, pulling her away from the plants. She screamed and bit me and went back to tearing up the yard. I ran to the house, fuming, calling out to Sheela to stop her, but Sheela just calmly asked, "What did you do to Naya? Why was she screaming?" Sheela pointed to Naya's mess and ordered me to "go clean that up at once."

I have never felt so alone and helpless. I found purpose in toiling and taking care of those plants. To have them ripped up and destroyed was like ripping my heart out and trampling on it. I had no solace. I had no voice. I really had nothing but my little red book and my bedroom.

3 • Cinderella

I stared at Sheela with contempt and suppressed anger. She stared back at me. That silent communication said to me, "You do as you are told." Kumar came over to me and helped me. Kumar had his good days, and by helping me, he could get back at his sister. That was all he cared about. All I knew was that it was nice having someone on my side for a change.

However, that did not last very long. I was seventeen when things got worse. One night, I woke up and found a member of that family in my bed … his hand on my most private part! I thought I was dreaming. My heart was pounding so hard I couldn't hear myself breathe. Why was he stroking me? I sat up in bed, and he ran off. I felt sick. I had no idea what was happening, but I convinced myself that it was all a dream and brushed it off. Being in denial is a beautiful thing.

I still cringe, and my heart still races when I think about that incident. Others have sexually abused me, but the first time is most shocking. A few weeks later, it happened again. I woke up to find him sitting on my torso, his hands on my breast. This time I grabbed his arms and pushed him off me. He ran off again. That night, I could not go back to sleep. I felt sick to my stomach. I went downstairs to the shower and washed his repulsive touch away. I sobbed quietly in the shower. Will this never end? Should I reveal this to the family? Will anyone believe me?

I went back to bed and finally fell into an unrestful sleep, dreaming of monsters chasing me. I woke up the following day and made up my mind to tell Sheela after school. As was customary, when I got home that day, Sheela ignored my greeting. I told her I needed to chat with her. She looked past me as if I did not exist. I went to my room and sobbed.

The next day, I cornered Sheela in the kitchen and blurted out that I was being touched inappropriately. I was shaking with anger and fear as I recounted the first time. I never got to the second time because she stopped and looked at me with disgust.

"Why are you making up stories?" she demanded. I stared at her, not understanding her question.

"Making up stories?" I asked.

She looked at me with disdain and hostility. "Do not make up stories about my family, and if you spread this rumor around, I will make your life a living hell."

That reaction sucked all the air out of my lungs and all the fight went out of me. It was useless to argue or to tell anyone. No one believed me anyway. I shuffled to my room and, for the first time, realized it was no longer my safe space. That family member never came to my room again, but he was perverted enough to cut a hole in the wall that separated our bedrooms. I made sure not to change my clothes when he was around. Such perversion and constant dodging went on for another year.

I started to think that was the extent of the sexual abuse until one hot, lazy, humid Saturday when I had dozed off downstairs in one of the hammocks and woke up to find another family friend standing over me. It was someone we all loved and knew very well. I smiled and said hi. He smiled back, and before I knew it, he jumped in the hammock with me. I struggled to get out as fear gripped me. Fear was not new to me, but this type of abuse was the worst so far. He put his hand over my mouth, and the other hand crept under my dress, grabbing between my legs. This incident is challenging for me to write

3 • Cinderella

about. I still feel that same raw fear and nausea, but these days I have learned how to get over it quickly and not let it paralyze me for days.

I bit his finger; he yelped and slapped me. I got up and ran upstairs to my room. I grabbed my New Testament to my chest and sobbed into my pillow. Is this my fault? What was I doing wrong to make these things happen to me? I talked to my imaginary friend, and I felt hope again. He was my only constant.

PRESENT MOMENT

I have never talked about this second abuse to anyone before. It still feels shameful and demoralizing. There was more to it before I bit his fingers, but I cannot write it out. It is too still painful. For the longest while, I kept it a secret because of my shame and humiliation and because I blamed myself for it.

As the saying goes, "we are only as sick as our secrets." Sharing this story has released me from shame. I know that it is not my fault. I was sexually abused, and I was utterly helpless to stop it or defend myself. Not only was I helpless to stop it, but I also lacked basic human support that we all need to be resilient through such a horrendous experience.

Do you have a secret? Is it eating away at you? One of the hardest lessons for me to learn about resilience is that I needed to stop keeping secrets. They are like anchors that weigh us down and drag us deeper and deeper into the ocean of despair and disempowerment. Believe it or not, those secrets define who we are because it is the *only* storyline that plays in our heads repeatedly.

My secret was shameful at first because I was not sure how people would react to it. To be honest, I never thought about what reaction I was looking for when I shared it with them. The outpouring of understanding was overwhelming. I realized that was all I needed: love and support. Sharing it as an author helps me purge even more. As I write this, I can let go of these demons that held me hostage for longer than they should have.

Once I shared my past, others opened up. It was amazing to me to find that I was not the only one going through this. There were, sadly, scores of others. Revealing secrets, sharing what holds us hostage, and purging together is one of the most beautiful aspects of our humanity. No one can relate to a perfect human being. The truth is, no one is perfect, so get over it. We are flawed human beings trying to navigate this world the best way we can. If perfection is what you are trying to portray to the world, everyone will eventually see through you. Trying to be a perfectionist is exhausting. Be vulnerable, be open, be honest; it will set you free.

Once you are free from your secrets, you can be yourself. Not being able to be me was the hardest part about keeping these secrets. I was convinced that I was broken and beyond repair. I was convinced there was no way I could encourage other people, given the shame and disgrace I was carrying like a load of bricks around on my shoulders.

I also suffered from imposter syndrome. You see, imposter syndrome is a pattern in which I doubted my accomplishments, skills, and talents and suffered from this continuous fear of being exposed as a fraud. For example, I always questioned why my husband, Chris, married me. How could he really love

3 • Cinderella

me? I am broken, and I do not know how to be a wife. One day he will find out!

Once I shared this with Chris and discovered that he didn't look at me as damaged goods, I overcame that hurdle. The junk was out of the trunk, and he reassured me he only married me for my looks. (Okay, kidding.) He reassured me that he loved me for the person that I am. I never thought I was kind and patient or that I love fiercely and protectively. Once he told me that, I realized that it is so true, I would give you the clothes off my back if you need them. I was shocked. Despite my brokenness and my secrets, I did not know that I was still a great friend, a good mom, and an awesome wife.

I hope that hearing about how I overcame this horrible shame will help you overcome your secrets and live life to the fullest. Be careful with whom you share your past and your secrets. Be sure that it will be those friends and family who will encourage you to help you build resiliency. Share with people who will walk through that fire with you in grace and love and, most importantly, without judgment.

We must live in the now and not the past. Sharing our secrets delivers us from the past and launches us into the now. We must live life in our current realities. We must also understand that it's okay to take it one day at a time. You see, once you have shared a secret and realize how freeing it is, it encourages you to share more and to purge until there is nothing left to hold you back. It changes your mindset and strengthens your resolve.

That is where resilience lives.

4

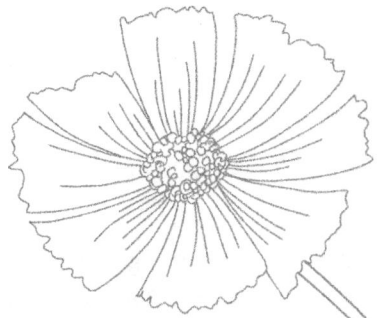

The Arranged Marriage

*"If you don't like something, change it.
If you cannot change it, change your attitude."*

—MAYA ANGELOU

LIFE CONTINUED, AND AT SEVENTEEN, I GRADUATED FROM high school. I was dreading what was to come after high school. I did not contemplate going to college, as I knew it was not an option. That did not bother me because, realistically, I knew that I could not afford it, and not many people in my country made it to college. I just needed a job to survive. The source of employment in my country was a sugar cane factory and a few sawmills. Fortunately for me, a family friend promised me a clerical job at the sugar cane factory.

I didn't have many safe places in my life, so high school was a safe haven for me. It was my getaway. I could pretend that I had a different life at high school. It was a place where no one knew the horror that I was living, and no one cared anyway. I needed my safe space so I could leave all my issues at home.

Back then, our high school was also interesting in the sense that boys and girls were segregated in class. They sat in separate sections. Because of this, we were socially awkward and did not know how to interact with the opposite sex. Since I was extremely extroverted, I was always in time-out in class. Time-out meant that my teacher paired me up to sit beside a boy. That was so painful for me at first, but it did not stop me from being a Chatty Cathy. It was how I met and got to know Liam. He was six feet tall—rare in my country—and had thick, black, curly hair and the most beautiful, kind, brown eyes. It was hard not to like him. I eventually started chatting with him, and we became friends.

Sanjay was very strict when it came to boyfriends or even just male friends. We were not allowed to interact with males. After not having friends or support for so many years, and with Liam giving me attention, I quickly became close to him, and we started dating. I use the term "dating" loosely because back then, dating in Guyana was sitting at the playground and talking, or walking home six or ten feet apart so that my uncle, who drove a taxi along the only road in our village, would not see us. It was impossible to hide anything in our small village.

The last year of high school was the best year of my life. I finally confided in Liam about what was going on in my life, and we promised each other that after we graduated high school, we would get married. For the first time, I felt loved and wanted. Even though I was terrified of Sanjay, I risked communicating with Liam on the weekends by sending notes in novels. Liam's friend would drop off the book under our gate with an aromatic note tucked inside. I would quickly get the note, write a reply, and plop the book right back under the gate. It was terrifying but exhilarating!

To say that I was over the moon when I graduated high school is an understatement. I was going to get a job as a clerk, save some money, and get married to Liam in a year. On the last day of school, Liam and I walked home together. Every time we saw a taxi in the distance, Liam would run ahead of me, and we would have fits of giggles. This was one of the happiest days of my life. Little did I know, my entire life was about to change within the blink of an eye on that same day.

Five minutes later, I arrived home to find Sheela and my Aunt Birdie (my mother's sister who played a small part in my life after my mother passed) sitting on the porch with a strange Guyanese man. He looked about eight to ten years older than I was. He was short, about 5' 8", and pale in complexion. He had a round face, and his brown eyes were squinty. His very short, curly, light-brown hair was neatly styled, and he had a mustache. As I slowly made my way to the porch, I heard Birdie say, "She is solid."

"Who is solid?" I wondered as I made my way toward them. Birdie got up as she saw me and pulled me toward the man and Sheela. My heart started racing; I knew something was wrong. Sheela was so happy and even hugged me. She was smiling at me and asked me how my day was. She *never* smiled at me, much less asked me how my day was. Sheela beckoned me to sit by her and proceeded to hold my hand. This woman had never touched me before. What the heck was happening? I started sweating profusely. She then told the man I was beautiful and good at cooking, cleaning, and washing. It dawned on me what was happening, and my world came crumbling around me. My heart was pounding so hard that all of their voices were drowned out by it.

You see, it is quite normal for men from my country to go abroad—especially to America—to establish themselves before coming back to Guyana to look for wives. In her quest to get rid of me—and in her words, "to do what was right for me"—Sheela was giving me away to this man. She said it was for my own good and that I had no future in Guyana. This was all true. I had no future in Guyana, but I knew her motive and it stung. It was all about getting rid of me, even if it meant giving me away to a stranger she knew nothing about.

I felt sick to my stomach as Sheela linked her hand in mine. It felt weird. I wanted to pull my hand away, but I sat there frozen. Aunt Birdie explained to me that I was getting married to this person in three days. They introduced him to me as Jay. They needed to start preparing for the wedding. I know that Aunt Birdie wanted what was best for me, but how could she think this was it? I was getting married in three days. That sentence kept playing over and over in my head. I sat there stunned. I never once looked at Jay.

It turned out that Jay's family had already planned my "wedding." There was no shortage of brides in Guyana for men coming back from abroad seeking wives. Jay knew he was in demand and that families were willing to offer up their daughters for a better life in America. I was brought back into reality as Birdie asked if I wanted to chat with Jay. I said no;

4 • The Arranged Marriage

I just wanted to go to my room. Jay seemed to be okay with that, and Birdie motioned for me to go. As I walked away, I heard Jay say sternly, "We are getting married in three days."

I barely made it to my room before my legs buckled and I collapsed on the floor. I started sobbing. I knew I had no voice, but this? This decision was made for me, and I was not even present when it was made. I knew this was traditional and normal in my country, but I never expected it to happen to me. I had plans for my life. Liam and I had plans. Then it hit me—Liam and me. What would happen to us? Did I have a choice in who I married? Could I say no to Birdie and Sheela? That thought never crossed my mind. I did not say no to anything, I just did as I was told. I started sobbing harder.

That evening, like clockwork, Liam's friend arrived to drop off our daily note. I covertly met with him and, through tears, told him what had happened. He promised to tell Liam everything as he rode off like a bat out of hell. He was not gone for twenty minutes before I saw Liam peddling his bike furiously up my street.

As he got closer to me, I could see his eyes were bloodshot and red, and his face was glistening with what I thought was sweat until he got closer to me. I realized it was both sweat and tears pouring down his cheeks. I signaled him to ride up the street, and I ran to meet him. He threw his bike on the ground and ran towards me, grabbing me and hugging me tightly. It was the first time we had ever hugged. It was my first hug *ever*. I never knew that hugs could feel so good. We both fell to our knees, still holding each other and sobbing.

I did not care that people were staring at us. Liam was there and all fears flew out the window for a few minutes. I did not care what would happen to me. All I knew was I wanted that moment to freeze in time, but we had no such luck. Nothing lasts forever. Liam got up and pulled me up with him.

"We need to go," he said.

"What do you mean?" I sobbed.

"I told my mother how I felt about you since the first day I met you, and she is fine with me bringing you to my house."

I looked up at him stupidly. "Bring me to your house? What do you mean? I am getting married in three days."

He started crying again. "I want you to run away with me, Silly."

I stared at him stunned. "Run away with you?"

The thought had never crossed my mind. My sister had run away with her boyfriend when she was fourteen years old. Sanjay had brought her back and had given her a severe beating. Nevertheless, she ran away again. It never crossed my mind to run away. I am good at learning from other people's mistakes, and I knew the consequences. I backed away from Liam, shaking my head.

"I cannot run away with you," I said. "I'm scared, and my family would kill me."

He looked at me, shocked. "What do you mean?"

"I am too scared," I said.

He slowly walked over to his bike, picked it up, turned around and looked at me. "Are you sure?" He asked.

I just stood there. I could not speak. He stared at me for a long time, leaned over, and kissed me on my cheek. Then he jumped on his bike and rode off. It was the last time I saw him. I used to wonder what it would have been like if I had taken him up on his offer. It took me a long time, but I finally understood that I probably would have ended up like so many women in my country at that time: married to a man who couldn't support his family because he was caught in the vicious cycle of alcoholism and joblessness, despite having five or six kids to support. It didn't mean that Liam was a bad guy or that we didn't love each other, but it's challenging to battle against cultural norms that don't allow you to win.

I ran all the way home. When I got to the house, I knew I would be prepped for my wedding day, meaning Ubtan would be massaged into my skin three times a day for the next two days. Ubtan is a yellow paste that is made with turmeric, flour, and rosewater. It is believed to make your skin flawless and glowing. It is customary for brides to be prepped this way in my culture. Somehow, the whole prepping felt sinister and ominous of what was to come. I had witnessed so many joyous weddings. I wished I could feel joy. I never really fantasized about what my wedding day would have looked like. I started crying again, sinking into a pit of hopelessness.

The next day, Jay came to visit me. As we sat on the couch, he tried to grab my hand, but I pulled away from him. He didn't ask me any questions about myself; he wasn't interested in me. However, Jay also did not mince words. He told me I was not allowed to work, and we would have a proper wedding in America. He said he would make sure I attended college once we arrived in America. It all seemed so factual. All the while he was speaking, I could not stop thinking about Liam. My heart was heavy, and as I thought about him, I started to cry. Jay seemed not to care or mind that I was crying. He sat there staring at me for what seemed like an eternity. Then he got up, patted my head, and left.

The ladies who were preparing me for the wedding ran in giggling. They were giddy with excitement about how handsome he was. They grabbed me and started applying more Ubtan on me. I finally broke my silence and asked one of the ladies if she knew who Jay and his family were.

She looked shocked. "Did you not ask him? Do you not know anything about him?"

I told her I was not interested in talking to him and that I did not want to get married to him.

She took a step back and looked at me with quizzical eyes. "You know that this is the best for you, right?"

I stared back at her. "Says who?" I demanded.

She came closer and whispered, "Sally, this is good for you. It is your future. You will be happy."

I sighed. I "will" be happy. It was like everyone was "willing" me to be happy. I knew there was no use trying to tell her otherwise. I had learned so much by watching how the people around me lived, and I wondered how marrying Jay could be worse. Maybe this *was* the best thing for me. If I knew what nightmare awaited me, I would have rethought that possibility.

The following day, Jay, Birdie, and I went to the court to acquire the marriage certificate. As we were signing it, I noticed Jay hesitated. Then he carefully drew, yes, he drew his signature on the certificate.

Birdie and I exchanged glances at each other. We realized he was completely illiterate. Jay caught our glimpses but was

4 • The Arranged Marriage

not fazed by them. As we left the building, I squeezed Birdie's hand and pulled her back.

"I don't want to marry him. He cannot read or write. I hate him already."

She looked at me and said firmly, "Sally, this is best for you."

Two days later, I was sitting around a fire, getting married in the Hindu wedding ceremony, swallowed in someone's borrowed wedding dress. I kept my head down during the entire ceremony. Everyone seemed to think that I was shy, but I was grieving. If Liam showed up, I vowed I would get up and run off with him right there and then. Oh, how I wished he would come back and sweep me away, but he didn't.

That night, Jay was very drunk when he came to bed. I was wearing an oversized blue nightgown that Birdie gave to me. She had told me with a mischievous wink that it would be an unforgettable night. I sat in the corner of the room on the floor, waiting. I was never told what to expect on my wedding night. I had never even kissed! We never had sex education in school, and sex was not discussed in our culture. It was taboo.

Suddenly the bedroom door burst open, and Jay rushed in. He looked around and started shouting my name. I cringed. I am used to alcoholics, and I instantly recognized he was an aggressive one. I slowly stood up from the floor.

"There you are," he said. "Now, take off your nightgown."

My heart jumped to my throat. "No," I said.

He smiled menacingly as he walked towards me. I backed into the wall and started shaking in fear. As he got close to me, I could smell his breath. It was stale with alcohol from drinking all day long. I turned my head away from his pungent breath. He reached out, grabbed me, threw me on the bed, and forced himself on me. The nightmare was over in two minutes.

He pushed me aside when he was finished and said, "Now you are mine, and I can do whatever I wish."

Long after he passed out, I curled up tightly in a ball and sobbed.

"Oh, Birdie. It *was* an unforgettable night. Here I am, out of the frying pan and into the fire," I said aloud as Jay snored beside me.

I felt sorry for myself. "What a pathetic life," I thought, and then suddenly, I was hit by an intense sensation rising inside me. A burning sensation rose from my toes to my head. I jackknifed into a sitting position as I realized it was rage. I had spent so much of my life feeling sorry for myself; I realized I never felt anything else. I was always the victim without a voice, without power, without strength.

I gritted my teeth and started talking to my imaginary friend. I vowed I would stand up for women one day, stand up for those who did not have a voice. For one brief, beautiful moment, I felt empowered, strong, and hopeful. For one brief, beautiful moment, I wasn't a victim. I lay my head down on the pillow and fell into a sweet sleep.

The abuse continued. It was not just sexual but physical and mental. As I had suspected, Jay was an abusive alcoholic, far worse than I had experienced so far. He drank every day for the next seven days and abused me every night. It was always "my fault." If it wasn't because he lost a fight with someone else, it was because I was not "woman enough" for him. Within a week, I learned that I was ugly, stupid, useless, and good for nothing. He told me that no one could love me the way he did, and if I tried to leave him, he would kill me.

Well, I thought to myself, if that was love, I do not want to experience what he would do to me if he hated me. Needless to say, I hated everything about him. A week later, I heaved a big sigh of relief as he returned to America and started my sponsorship. It took three years for my sponsorship to be finalized. During those three years, Jay would visit Guyana annually, and the abuse continued.

As my visa was being processed during the final year, I begged Sheela and Birdie not to send me to America with Jay.

"He'll kill me," I said, sobbing. "You have no idea what he is doing to me."

I was told I was damaged goods because I was no longer a virgin and no one else would want me. Maybe if I were good to Jay, he would be good to me. I needed to learn how to be a good wife. I started having suicidal thoughts again. This time, though, I fully understood what those thoughts meant. I was no longer eight years old, wondering why I could not go to sleep forever. I was twenty years old and knew I did not want to live.

PRESENT MOMENT

I know I am not the only woman that went through such a horrific marriage experience. I also know many of you are still stuck or forced to stay in abusive marriages and think that there is no way out.

However, amidst my adulterated hell of a wedding night, I found my calling. I knew in my heart of hearts that one day I would stand up for women because I would no longer be a victim. I knew that one day, I would find my resiliency to be bold and brave. While it took me years and years to find my voice and resilience, that night, my God-given calling emerged and hit me like a bolt of lightning. While it was a brief moment of clarity, that clarity seared my soul forever. I had something to offer to the world. I had my story, which I knew would be the driving force to deliver someone else from an abusive situation.

While this chapter is horrifying in and of itself, it taught me to look outside of myself and my current situation and to know I could go on with a purpose, no matter what. So can you. You will find your resiliency and your strength when you find your purpose.

It matters what you are going through, and it matters why you are reading this book. If you have gotten this far, I hope you continue to read, as I know this book will resurrect the driving force within you to take back what is rightfully yours: your power.

You take your control back when you decide to start talking to someone about what you are going through. Talk to people who you know can advise and support you. See a professional who can help you. Depending on what you are going through, get the right tools to help yourself.

Learn how to set boundaries and maintain those boundaries but be sure that you will be safe while doing so. I would have been dead had I tried to put limits in place when I was in the midst of my trial. Do not put yourself in that situation. You know your situation better than I do, so use your judgment.

I love this quote by Brené Brown: "I want to be in the arena. I want to be brave with my life. And when we make the choice to dare greatly, we sign up to get our asses kicked. We can choose courage, or we can choose comfort, but we can't have both. Not at the same time."

Remember, no one has the right to take away your power. They can only take it if you give it to them. But taking your power back and holding on to it takes bravery and—sometimes—getting your ass kicked. It takes stepping out of your comfort zone and stepping into a life of resilience and boldness.

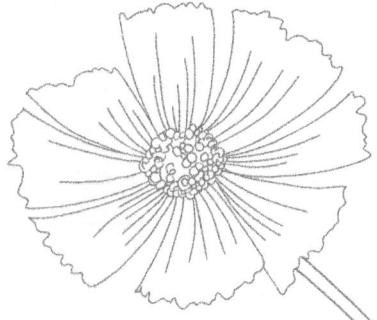

5

Coming to America

"A mother's love for her child is like nothing else in the world. It knows no law, no pity. It dares all things and crushes down remorselessly all that stands in its path."

—AGATHA CHRISTIE

THREE YEARS AFTER THE WEDDING, I FOUND MYSELF getting on a plane to America.

A few weeks before I departed, I tried to reach Liam, but he refused to see me. I was heartbroken but did not blame him. How could I be upset? After all, he tried to rescue me, but I rejected him and his offer.

One of the hardest things I have ever done in my life—to this day—was to get on that plane to America. I knew what was in store for me: a level of abuse that most people could not even conceive. In this new country that was supposed to be the "land of opportunity," I had no friends, no family. I knew if I were to be killed—a real possibility—no one would ever know.

I landed in New York in September, 1993.

As the plane started to descend, I looked out the window. I had never seen so many lights in my life. I grew up in a village without electricity. I gazed at the beautiful, glittering New York City, and suddenly, I had hope. Maybe this *was* a land full of opportunities. I felt my spirits lifted. I could make this work. I could have a life with Jay. Perhaps he would not drink as much here. After all, when he visited Guyana, he was always on holiday. I felt my spirit soared and I felt hopeful, but that was short lived.

A family member gave us a ride home since Jay did not drive. The car ride home was quiet. No conversation. I was okay with that. I felt awkward and intimidated around men anyway. I felt it keenly that I had no voice—that part of my culture had traveled with me with no problem at all.

Once we arrived at the house, Jay took me to our bedroom. Even before the door was closed, he grabbed me by the neck and held me up against the wall. He stared into my eyes and he said to me in the most menacing voice I had ever heard, "If you ever try to leave me, I will kill you. Don't think that you will ever be smarter than me. You are never going to college. You do as you are told, and you get to live."

He released me, and I dropped to the floor in defeat. All my hopes for a happy life flew out the window.

5 • Coming to America

A month later, I was pregnant. I was scared out of my mind. I had no idea what that would mean for me, but it was easy to see what Jay was doing. A child would be his collateral. If we had a child together, it would be harder for me to run from him.

During that time, Jay found a job for me at a drugstore. My routine was to wake up at 4:00 a.m., cook (Jay needed fresh food daily), get to work, and get back home. I was not allowed to have friends, stay out late, or do anything else. Once, I tried to shave my legs, and Jay went into a rage I did not understand at the time. He slapped me hard and asked me whom I was shaving my legs for. It took me years to realize that forbidding me to shave my legs had nothing to do with him thinking that I was trying to attract other men; it had to do with him controlling me and taking away my power by not giving me basic control over my body.

As I settled into my new life, I started noticing a pattern. We lived in a house with other family members. The men's routine was straightforward: to work all week and get drunk all weekend. They were all aggressive drunks and sometimes would beat the heck out of each other on the weekends. Then all was okay during the week. Violence was nothing new to me and was normal; by now, I think I expected it. I had given up hope that my life would be anything else but always in this sad state of affairs. However, I was not giving up on Jay and me. I could make this work.

I started to notice that when Jay was not around his family, he drank less. I thought if Jay were out of the house away from them, maybe this dysfunctional marriage could work after all. It took me months to muster up the courage to share this with Jay. I never saw it coming. No sooner than the words were out of my mouth, he threw me up against the wall and started hitting me.

"I will never leave my parents' home!" he shouted. "How dare you accuse my family of having a bad influence on me?"

I never brought up the subject again, but I hoped that I would have the courage to leave one day, and if and when I did, I would never look back.

I had seen a vicious cycle in my village growing up. Women went in and out of bad relationships. They just kept coming back. I understood at the time that they had no choice. They had no way of making money or providing for themselves and their children. But remember what I said a few chapters before this one? I learn from other people's mistakes. That was why I knew if I ever got the courage to leave Jay, there would be no cycle. That would be the end of that vicious cycle for me. I would not be a statistic.

Nine months into my pregnancy, I woke at 4:00 a.m. as usual and was cooking when the first contraction hit me. I gasped and grabbed my abdomen. I am 4' 10", and it turns out I was carrying an eight-pound baby. The pain came sporadically all day, and by 6:00 p.m., we knew it was time for me to go to the hospital. I was terrified. I had no idea what to expect. Jay thought Lamaze class was a waste of time and money.

We arrived at the hospital around 7:00 p.m. I labored from then until 3:00 a.m. without an epidural. The doctors said that something was wrong with the baby and that they could not administer any medication. Most of those eight hours were a blur. Finally, my son, Richard, was born. I never saw him that day, and I passed out until the following day.

5 • Coming to America

The next day, the nurse came over and handed me this little bundle of joy. I stared at him as he slept peacefully. "What will your life look like, little boy?" I thought.

The nurse gently tapped my shoulder and asked me if I picked out a name. I looked at her with a blank stare. She said, "Perhaps you want to wait until his father is back?"

I shook my head vehemently. "No, I want to name him."

Jay had already picked out a name that I hated. After going through that many hours of labor without medication, I was going to name my baby. I told the nurse to put Richard on the birth certificate. I always loved that name. It was an act of defiance, and it gave me strength.

A month later, I was back to work at the drugstore. Because I love makeup, the boss put me to work at the makeup counter. I loved helping customers. One day, a recurring customer pulled me aside. She whispered, "You are brilliant and have great customer service ethics. Why are you working at this drug store?"

I told her I did not have a college degree and just a high school diploma from my country and did not think I could do better. She told me that she worked at a bank and encouraged me to stop by and pick up an application. She said I did not need a college degree for a job as a bank teller. I told her I would consider it.

A few weeks later, I mustered up the courage and visited the bank. I got the application and filled it out. Three weeks later, I got the job. I was terrified to tell Jay, but I did anyway. I sold the job to him by telling him that I would be making more money for our future. Jay seemed okay with that. By then, I was managing the little money that we had. Jay worked at a picture-frame factory and barely made enough to cover his drinking habit and bills, so it didn't take a lot of convincing.

Three years later, nothing much had changed. Jay was as abusive as ever. Richard, at three years old, was unruly. Because I went back to work one month after his birth, I never bonded with him. I felt no maternal instincts, and all I really did when I was home was discipline him and teach him manners. Some days I wondered why God gave me this child. I had no idea how to be a mother. I was "dragged up" with no one as a role model. Jay had no idea how to be a father, either.

My daily routine was the same as before, except now I sat in the train station, counting the trains and wondering which one I should jump in front of. I did this daily, continually contemplating my demise. I just wanted to die. I had nothing to live for.

Some days, I fantasized about leaving Jay. I knew I should leave him, but where would I go? I did not have enough money. Jay made sure I did not learn how to drive, and what about Richard? What about this little boy? How would I take care of him? I felt an intense sense of desperation. I was in a deep depression, but that did not last long. A week later, I learned why this little boy came into my life.

On this particular night, Jay was so drunk that I knew that he was in a dangerous state of mind. I knew this stage well. I lived in it for so many years. The weather seemed to match his moods and, it was pouring rain. Lightning flashed across the sky as thunder raged loudly. I knew that this was yet another premonition. Something terrible was about to happen.

5 • Coming to America

As Jay walked into the room, I could smell the alcohol from the doorway. Oh crap, I thought as I closed my eyes tightly and pretended to be asleep. I felt him standing over me, breathing heavily. I shut my eyes tightly and held my breath. I was afraid he would hear my heart pounding.

I heard him walk away and breathed a sigh of relief. It was short-lived. A few seconds later, I nearly jumped out of my skin as he started to blast music. I flew into a sitting position, my heart racing even faster. Richard, startled by the music, had started crying as well. I walked over to Richard's bed and tried to soothe him back to sleep, but he began screaming louder.

Jay walked over to me, grabbed me, and dragged me to the middle of the floor.

"Dance with me!" He shouted over the music.

I was terrified but furious at the same time. I looked at the clock and it was 2:00 a.m. I stood still. He grabbed my waist and tried to get me to move, but I did not budge. Suddenly, I was no longer scared. I felt wave after wave of anger wash over me. It took everything I had not to scream over the music: "How dare you? I am so tired of this crap."

On the inside, I *was* screaming, "F*** you, Jay. Kill me if you want. But F*** you."

I stepped back and pushed him as hard as I could. He fell to the ground and stared at me in disbelief. That was a bad idea. Never lay hands on a violent drunk. He got up slowly. I could see his eyes narrowing and his breath quickening. I knew I was in for it, and all my anger dissipated. I ran to Richard, grabbed him, and ran to the door.

Jay caught me by the hair and pulled me back. He grabbed Richard and threw him on the bed. He then shoved me to the floor and started to strangle me. I clawed at his hands as I struggled to breathe. His face swam before my eyes. I felt myself passing out as I saw Richard standing over him with the remote control in his hand. He smacked Jay on the shoulder, screaming at him, "Leave my mommy alone! Don't hurt my mommy!"

Finally, Jay relented and relaxed his grip on my neck, only to turn around and swat Richard like a fly. Richard flew across the room, crashed into the dresser, and lay there still, whimpering.

Both Jay and I stared at each other in shock. Finally, I mustered my strength and shoved Jay off of me. I ran over to Richard, screaming his name over and over again. I also saw the look of horror on Jay's face as he walked to where Richard was. I shoved him out of the way as I picked up my son. He was so tiny, so helpless, so fragile—so innocent. Tears were streaming down his little face.

Something broke inside of me. It was like a floodgate was thrown open and my heart was broken for Richard. Up until that moment, I had never felt any maternal instinct. I was so focused on myself and lived in survival mode for so long that I did not know that I was capable of feeling anything for anyone, even my child. However, at that precise moment, I knew what the term "mama bear" meant, and I embraced and clung to that feeling because I knew it was going to be my lifeline.

I heaved and heaved as I was consumed by the feeling of love for my son. My chest constricted, and I thought I was going to have a heart attack. It took me less than a minute to realize that I could not live without this little boy. I would die for him. Right at that moment, I realized my son was the only

5 • Coming to America

human being I had ever loved, and he was not going to grow up in this environment. I decided right then and there that I was going to run away. I was unsure how and when, but I was going to do it. The big revelation that gave me almost superhuman strength was that I had to do it for him.

This tiny four-year-old had restored my faith and hope in myself. This part of my story was going to be for him. Of that, I was certain.

―――――― PRESENT MOMENT ――――――

What would you do for someone you love? To what lengths would you go to protect him or her? Until this moment in my life, I never thought I could live a life of resiliency. I was confined in a box that was created by others. My confinement was built with lies of how weak, ugly, and stupid I was. The most robust wall holding my box in place was that I would never amount to anything because I was damaged goods. This was a lifetime of lies that compounded and left me in a state of fear, insecurity, and low self-esteem.

The big question is, did I gain courage and resilience overnight? The answer is no. Courage and resilience lived inside me all my life. I just needed the inspiration to activate it.

Do you see where I am going with this? I know that we are all resilient and courageous. Sometimes we just have to dig deep to find that part of ourselves. In my case, my son restored my faith in myself as a mother and as a woman. He saved my life that night. Seeing his little helpless body curled up against the dresser snapped me out of that victimized mindset. My role was to protect him. I knew that I needed to get this little boy out of the toxic environment we lived in, no matter what else

I did. Richard should not get used to living in such a hostile and abusive home. I never had a safe space, and I realized that I wanted one for him.

He needed a safe place where he could be a kid and not worry about me. He needed a space where he felt safe, protected, and loved. That motivated me.

A person who is motivated to change is resilient. That motivation isn't half-assed, either. It has to come from the very depth of your soul. It has to *mean* something. An addict cannot become sober until they decide to change fundamentally. If they don't make that decision, they won't change. Why? Because they aren't motivated.

Find your motivation and you find your core resiliency. It's that simple. And that profound.

6

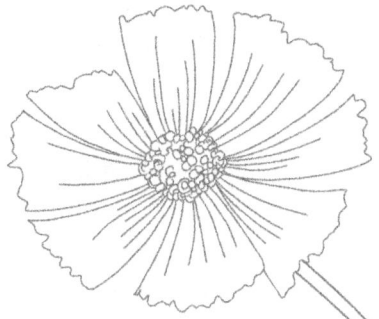

The Great Escape

"If you run, you stand a chance of losing, but if you don't run you've already lost."

—BARACK OBAMA

I HAD REASON TO LIVE AGAIN. I NO LONGER SAT AT THE TRAIN station waiting to jump in front of an oncoming train. I had a purpose, mission, and vision. I had a sweet little boy to live for, and I needed to find a way to protect him. However, I knew that in order to protect him, I needed to be brave and strong.

By now, I was starting to see myself for who I was, and I did not like that person. I had no self-esteem, I was a people pleaser, and I was insecure. I could not even make eye contact when I interacted with people.

Since I was determined to be bold and brave, I knew that I had to make eye contact so that I could project confidence. I needed to if I were going to live on my own. Fortunately, I worked at a bank and had to interact with lots of customers daily. So I practiced. At first, I would make eye contact for a second but then quickly ducked my head. After a week, the eye contact lasted for two seconds. After a month, I realized that I could make eye contact for the entire duration that the customer was at my window. I no longer ducked my head or cowered. That was one of the most empowering things I have ever done.

Next, I knew that I needed to learn how to use the computer and learn Microsoft Office to get a better-paying job to support Richard and me. I did my research and started taking computer and Microsoft Office courses. I lied and told Jay that I was working overtime. I do not advocate lying, but it was for the greater good—survival in this case. I was starting to feel empowered as I kept pressing on and stepping out into bravery. I could feel my resilience growing and getting stronger.

The next step was confiding in someone. Opening up was a *huge* deal for me because, up until that point, I never had a safe space or anyone that I could trust and confide in. This next step was terrifying, but I knew if I were going to run away, I could not do it alone. I did not know how to navigate in this country. Heck, I did not know how to navigate life! Plus, I did not drive and therefore did not own a car. I had never been out of the state of New York, where we resided. I was only going from work to home. I had a lot going against me.

One day, I was sitting in the lunchroom at work, contemplating who I should trust, when Izzy walked in. Izzy was petite and cute. She always had this twinkle in her eyes. I always admired how she carried herself with confidence. I secretly admired and respected her but was also very intimidated by her. Izzy was always kind to me. On that day, she sat down beside me and looked me squarely in the eye. I wanted to look away but locked eyes with her.

"Why is your cheek red?" She asked.

My hand flew to my cheek and covered it defensively. I was embarrassed because it was from yet another "incident" at home. She took my hand and held it. That was all I needed. The floodgates opened up. I sobbed and sobbed. I barely saw people coming in and out of the break room. I was purging, and it felt great. That evening, we went to dinner, and I shared everything with Izzy.

I was surprised that she cried with me; she hugged me tightly and told me that everything would be okay. For the first time, I truly believed that. Izzy was my first experience with a support system, a sister, the beginning of my tribe.

Next, I got an attorney, Mr. Caste. Mr. Caste was a customer with our bank. I told him my story, and he promised to represent me for free. Funny, Mr. Caste noticed that I was forcing myself to make eye contact with him. He was a daily customer and watched my struggle over time. He was proud of me and offered to help me with anything I needed. I was overwhelmed. I wish I had been brave enough to do this three years before, but God's timing is perfect. I knew that *He* was looking out for me. I, of course, had never stopped chatting with my imaginary friend through the entire ordeal, and I knew that I had the best friend I could ever hope for to help me—but I also knew that God knew that I was finally ready.

Six months after I started planning our escape, I only had two more pieces of the puzzle I needed to solve before executing my plan. I needed a better-paying job and a place to live. I had no idea where to start or what to do, but fate intervened. One bright Monday morning, one of my favorite customers, Bruce, asked me out for coffee. Bruce and his team liked how I treated them as customers. They had a job opening and he wanted me to work for them. The only skill needed was Microsoft Office. Are you ready for this? The salary was almost twice as much as I was making annually. It was a no-brainer. Without hesitating, I said yes.

Three weeks later, I started my new job. I did not share this with Jay since the new job was in the same building as the bank; he had no way of finding out. When I started working at the bank, I managed all our money. He was so arrogant and believed that he had frightened and terrorized me so much that I would never defy him. He was also very confident that I would never leave him.

I had almost everything that I needed to leave, but then I started second-guessing myself. I played all the scenarios in my head about what would happen if I were caught, and I became very fearful. None of those scenarios played out well. As abusive as Jay was, I wanted to give him one more chance because of Richard—and okay, let me be honest, I was scared to leave him. I was scared of him, and I was afraid to be on my own.

So I gave him one more chance to see if he would be willing to leave his family's house and get our own place. I waited until he was sober and in a good mood to broach the subject. This time I took a different approach. I told him that I wanted more time with him, me, and Richard. I would like the three of us to spend the weekends together and go out and do stuff as a family.

Jay looked at me as if I had grown three heads.

"More time with you?" He laughed, but it had no humor. "You are stupid. I will spend more time with my son and my family. I do not need you; you need me. You can never leave me. No one will want you."

Then he dragged me to the front door and challenged me to leave. Could this be it? Is he really allowing me to leave?

As I got to the door, he blocked it, lunged at me, and shoved me against the wall.

"I will find you and kill you if you try to leave," he whispered in my ear.

There it was, my last attempt—his last chance. I knew that I would never ask him again to leave with me. His reaction was not only terrifying but downright humiliating. The next day, I was on the train heading into work. Once again, I could see no light at the end of the tunnel as to where I would live. How could I run away? I did not even know where and how to look for an apartment. I called on my imaginary friend and pleaded with Him for help. By now, I understood that all these years, I had been praying. Jesus had been and still was my anchor. Talking to Him kept me sane.

As I was leaving the train, I heard a voice saying, "Look up Sally." I looked up and saw an advertisement right across the aisle from where I was sitting. My heart started racing. Could it be true? I stayed on the train and did not care that I missed my stop. I read the ad repeatedly. It was for an apartment building located on the border of New York and New Jersey. It had everything I needed. There was a bus that shuttled residents from the apartment complex to Manhattan, where I worked. A grocery store was in the complex, and a kindergarten, elementary, and middle school was across the street. This was everything that I needed. Since I did not have time and money to learn how to drive, this apartment complex was perfect, almost too good to be true.

I could not sleep that night. I tossed and turned all night as my thoughts raced and bounced around in my head. It was a gated community with guards posted at the gate 24/7. Jay would not have access to me. This was too good to be true. I kept replaying the ad in my head. I felt feverish and sick to my stomach the next day, but I was determined to get more information about this apartment complex.

I skipped work and took the bus to New Jersey. I trembled during the entire ride. I could barely walk after I got off the bus. Somehow, I made it to the building and was greeted by Sue. Sue was about 5' tall with curly brown hair and the greenest, wisest set of eyes I had ever seen. Sue could tell that I was nervous, and after I asked about the security and the guard for the fifth time, she took my hands, looked into my eyes, and asked, "Who are you running from, Honey?"

I stared at her, wide-eyed. I could not speak. How did she know? My thoughts raced. I pulled my hands away from hers, but she grabbed my hands again.

"I don't want to pry into your business, but I can help if you are running from someone dangerous."

I nodded my head, and Sue walked me to her office. I told her that I was running from my husband. I quickly assured her that he was not dangerous, but I also told her in all honesty that he would kill me if he found me.

She smiled. "And you say he is not dangerous?"

I muttered, "I mean, he hits me, but he has not killed anyone. So I guess he is not dangerous."

She looked at me kindly. "Honey," she said. "That man should be behind bars for hitting a precious little thing like you."

Me? Precious? I snickered. She looked at me quizzically.

I blurted out, "I know that I am not brave, but I just need to do this for my son."

She looked at me sadly. I wondered what was going through her head. Looking back now, I see how stupid my comments were. I was being abused, and I was exhibiting the classic signs of denial.

Sue processed my lease that day, and I walked out with the keys to my new apartment. I could not return to work that day, so I went straight to Central Park in New York City. I found a quiet, secluded spot and parked myself there. I took the key out of my purse and kissed it, my ticket to freedom. Then I broke down and sobbed until I had nothing left.

As I write this, I picture that girl crying under the tree in the park, and my heart still aches. At that time, I did not know why I was purging. I realized I cried in relief, but I was also crying because I was afraid. What if I was a bad mom? What if I did not know how to take care of my son? What if something happened to him? I was starting to make excuses as to why I should put off escaping once again.

When I got home, I made sure that I hid the key deep in my purse. I knew that Jay did spot checks on my wallet. I was restless and afraid to leave the room. The next morning, I went to work and told Izzy what I had done. She was thrilled and wanted to know when I planned on moving. I told her that I had not set a date.

I wasn't sure if I would ever set that date to execute my plan; even though I had no excuses, I kept making crap up. However, I believe that everything happens for a reason. That weekend, I found the courage to confront Jay, because he was allowing Richard to take puffs from his cigarette and sips from his beer bottle. He was furious at me because I was defiant with other people around.

As I was walking away from him, he grabbed me, spun me around, and slapped me several times. He had never hit me in front of anyone. I was so embarrassed, but my resolve strengthened as I walked away. This time I did not cry, nor did I feel sorry for myself. This time I went to my purse, pulled out the key to my new apartment, and made up my mind. I was leaving tomorrow, which was a Monday. Jay and everyone else would be at work.

Before going to bed that night, I told Jay that I had a day off from work the next day and would stay home. While he was asleep, I wrote him a long letter as to why I was leaving. The following day, after he left for work, I threw my and my son's clothes in a laundry bag. It was all I needed. I left the letter and Mr. Caste's business card on the neatly made bed.

I told Richard that we were going to the laundromat. He was excited. He loved the laundromat. I was shaking in my sneakers. Okay, I have never been so scared in my life. Jay's

6 • The Great Escape

parents were home. I tried to sneak out quietly but heard his mom calling my name. I froze. She rushed to the door.

"Are you going out?" She asked.

I swallowed the lump of fear in my throat.

"Yes," I answered. "Laundry."

She looked at the bag and then at me.

"Oh, then buy me a gallon of milk."

I almost peed myself in relief!

"Sure," I said and rushed out the door, Richard flying behind me.

I dumped the laundry bag in a cart so I could move faster, grabbed Richard's hand, and ran with the cart and Richard two blocks away from the house. As soon as we were out of sight, I called a cab. Richard was puzzled.

"Why do we need a cab, Mom?"

I told him that we were going on an adventure. He was ecstatic.

I waited impatiently for the cab; my entire body was quaking. Richard asked if I was cold. I could not speak. It was May, so it was nice and warm that day. All I could think about was, would I make it? Was Jay watching? Did he believe that I had a day off? Were his parents calling him? Suddenly I felt bile rising in my throat, and I could not keep it down. I started vomiting. The stress was too much. Richard looked at me in alarm, but thankfully the cab pulled up at that moment. I grabbed a towel from the laundry bag, wiped my mouth, and hopped in.

This was surreal. I could not believe it was happening. Perhaps I was dreaming. I pinched myself several times. I even pinched Richard once. He yelped, and I smiled. It was the sweetest sound. I could not believe that we were free at last. Richard was excitedly chattering about all the trucks and busses that were passing by. I looked at him. His little face beamed, and my fear slowly dissipated. I was doing this for him. I could never do it for myself. I was so complacent and blind to anything outside of my box; I had blinders on. He gave me strength, and he opened my eyes because he deserved a better life. I refused to let him be a victim of my past.

Richard was excited about our new apartment.

"Mom, Mom, look," he shouted as he ran around, sliding on the veneer flooring.

I realized that I was smiling. I could not remember when I had last smiled in his presence. I caught him as he slid towards me and gave him a big hug.

"Let's go shopping," I told him.

We walked to the store. I bought two of everything that I thought we would need, including a comforter and two pillows. Then we called a cab and went home. Around 6:00 p.m., my phone started ringing, and Richard began to cry. He wanted to go home to his dad, and his dad wanted to talk to me on the phone.

Fear and panic set in again. I had no one here to talk to me. I had left a message for my friend Izzy, but I knew I wouldn't hear from her until the next day. I fed Richard, and he finally fell asleep on the makeshift bed on the floor. I looked at him sleeping peacefully on the floor and broke down. What had I done? He had a real bed at home. I lay down beside him, still sobbing until I eventually passed out.

6 • The Great Escape

The next day, I woke up disoriented and sore. I looked around, and then I remembered. This was not a dream; I was at my new place and I had thirty voicemails on my mobile phone. As I listened to them, fear built up again. The messages started with Jay begging me to come back home, then they turned to threats, and eventually, he started cursing me and yelling death threats. He threatened to call the cops because I had kidnapped Richard and ran off.

I deleted all the messages for fear that I would listen to them again and go into a tailspin. Then I ran to the bathroom and threw up. Finally, after about thirty minutes, I composed myself and took a shower. I woke up Richard, gave him some breakfast, and went to meet his new babysitter. Richard was still asking about going home and wanting his dad. I was at a loss as to what to say to him.

That same day, I filed for divorce. Mr. Caste told me that he spoke with Jay and that Jay was backing off and would leave us alone. He would also not be reporting Richard as kidnapped, as Mr. Caste had made it very clear to Jay that the police would want to know why I ran away with Richard. I told Mr. Caste that if Jay signed the divorce papers without a fight, I would make it an amicable separation and give him visitation. Jay agreed to sign, but I did not trust him. I know that it was not over. As much as I would like to say that it was a wrap, it was not. The saga continued.

Three weeks after my great escape, Jay followed me from work to my bus station. I was sitting in the back of the bus with my eyes closed when I felt someone plopped down beside me. My eyes flew open because this person was so close to me that I could smell the alcohol on his breath. I gasped and forgot to breathe as I stared at Jay. I tried to scream for the bus driver to stop, but nothing came out except a croak. I could tell that Jay was furious. He grabbed my arm and squeezed it hard.

"Shut up," was all he said.

Richard was ecstatic to see his father and could not wait to show him the new apartment. Jay seemed impressed. After the grand tour, I asked him to leave. He looked surprised.

"No. Why would I leave? You wanted us to have our place, and now we do. I just need to get my things."

I stood there dumbfounded. "Get your things?" I thought. "I just filed for a divorce." I sent Richard to his room and shut the door.

"You need to leave now," I said. "The divorce is being processed."

He walked threateningly towards me.

"What are you hiding? Exactly why did you leave me? I was a good husband, and I provided for you. I treated you well." He then ran to my room and burst open the closet door. "Who else is living here?"

Richard heard the commotion and ran out of his room. Jay looked at Richard and shouted again, "Who else is living here? Did your mom bring another man here? It is the only reason why she would leave me. She is cheating on me with another man."

I knew where this was going. I saw the signs. Jay had lost it and was in denial as to why I left him. I could sense the danger as he stepped towards me. I ran over to the phone and picked it up.

6 • The Great Escape

"I will call the police if you take one step closer to me!" I shouted.

He stopped. I had never done this before. With all the years of abuse, I dared not call the police. I knew the consequence would be dire. Calling the cops was a no-no, but this was a different ball game. I was no longer held in the bondage of the abuse. This was my safe space, and I would be damned if I let him invade it and violate it.

We stood there squared off, the phone as my defense. I could see him trying to figure out if I was brave enough to dial 911. He called my bluff and took another step towards me. With trembling fingers, I dialed. His jaw dropped.

"How dare you? You left me for another man and kidnapped my son, and now you are calling the cops?"

He lunged towards me, I grabbed Richard and I ran to the bedroom and locked the door. Richard started screaming.

I hung up as I heard the operator saying, "911 Emergency, how can I help you?"

Jay was still pounding the door when the phone rang. It was the 911 operator wanting to know why I called. I put the phone on speaker, and the pounding stopped. I could hear Jay's ragged breathing. Then I heard his footsteps receding, and the front door slammed. He was gone.

I told the operator that I called in error.

"Ma'am," she said. "Why is the child screaming?"

I told her there was a threat, but he left. She said she was sending the police anyway. I begged her not to, and I told her what happened. She advised me to get a restraining order.

I went to see Mr. Caste the following day and got the restraining order. The next week, we arranged the first visitation. Jay was supposed to pick up Richard at the train station since he was not supposed to know where I lived, but since I had blown my cover, I hoped that the restraining order would keep him away.

The first visitation went smoothly, and Richard was happy to see his father. I kept my distance from him. Dropping Richard off was a different story. Every time Richard returned, he was a hot mess. He would sulk for days. I noticed that he was turning from a sweet little boy into an angry five-year-old. I tried to talk to him, but he had shut down.

Even to this day, when I think of why he had shut down, I shiver and cringe. My little boy could not express his feelings about what was going on because it was too much for his little mind to handle. After three months of visitation, I finally threatened to stop Richard from going to his father's house if he didn't tell me what went on during his visitations. He finally broke down sobbing.

"I love you, Mom. I will never hurt you." He said this repeatedly.

I felt chills going up and down my spine. I still feel chills as I write this almost twenty years later.

"Richard, why would you hurt me?" I whispered.

He hugged my neck tightly. "Someone at my dad's house told me that I should take a knife and cut your throat when you were sleeping. I do not want to. I love you, Mom. I will never hurt you."

6 • The Great Escape

My heart constricted. I felt rage, the same rage I felt that night when Richard was thrown up against the wall. I wanted to hurt someone.

"Where was your dad when this happened?" I asked.

"He was sitting right there, and they all laughed."

I told Richard to get me a glass of water. As soon as he was gone, I grabbed a pillow and screamed into it.

When Richard came back, I asked him what else they were doing that was upsetting him.

"We watch grown-up movies."

"What's a grown-up movie, Rich?"

"You know, the ones that are with naked people."

Naked people? Apparently, he was watching porn movies with his cousins, who were only a few years older than he was. Jay appointed them babysitters.

The following week, I confronted Jay. He was furious and said that Richard was lying.

"Why would a five-year-old make up this crap?" I demanded.

Jay would not take responsibility. I threatened to stop visitation if Richard was left alone again with his cousins.

Mr. Caste recommended that Richard get professional help. Richard started seeing a psychologist. Things began to settle down, and Richard seemed to be getting well and coping better.

But there is always the calm before the storm.

PRESENT MOMENT

Nothing is better than a mission and a plan to galvanize a person into action. Protecting Richard was my mission. I knew that I needed an action plan for his survival. It doesn't matter what we are going through; we can have a mission. We know that mission is a good one when the action plan naturally and abundantly follows. My planning took a long time. As I prepared, I was building resiliency, even when I was fearful and did not see the light at the end of the tunnel.

I do not know where you are in life or where you are going, but I know one thing for sure, that you must prepare for what you want. When I took computer and Microsoft Office courses, I did not know what opportunities would come my way, but I knew that I needed to do my part to get to that next stage in life.

What can you do right now if you are in a holding pattern? How can you prepare for that moment of opportunity? Will you be ready? Will you take the chance when it presents itself to you?

I believed that Jay was my safety net, and he had convinced me that I could not survive without him. I convinced myself that I would fail without his help. Listen, I know that I am not the only woman who made up reasons and excuses not to do what was best for me. Now, let us be honest, am I alone? Anybody with me? We find all sorts of reasons to stay in our comfort zone, don't we? But let's not be hard on ourselves. You see, it was so ingrained in me that I could not do anything on my own that I never trusted myself.

Know that you can trust yourself. You are more resilient than you think. Learn from my mistakes the way I learned from the mistakes of others.

6 • The Great Escape

Next, if you do not have a fortress around you, you will fail. I am not talking about putting up walls around you; I mean getting your *tribe* to fortify you and to be that sounding board and strength you need. For the longest while, I only had my thoughts and the voices in my head, and it was the same mantra: You will never amount to anything. You will never stand on your own two feet.

Albert Einstein is credited with saying that insanity is doing the same thing over and over again, while expecting different results. That was how my thoughts were. Negative voices in my head were repeatedly playing. It was all I was used to. I was ugly, stupid, and I would never make it on my own because I was damaged goods.

Confiding in my friend Izzy and accepting help from Mr. Caste was a game-changer. They showed me a different perspective. They opened my eyes to how hard I was trying. They told me that my life was worth living because everyone deserves a fighting chance. They also said that what I was going through was not normal. Just because it was cultural did not make it normal. They helped me see that I was beautiful, kind, smart, and strong. This support gave me a new perspective that changed my mindset and helped me change my narrative. This new mindset was another pivot point in my life.

Because of this new understanding, I continued to build resiliency. Resiliency empowered me to plan and execute the great escape. Even though I was terrified, I knew that I had strength and support and that I would be okay.

And sure enough … I was. Eventually.

7

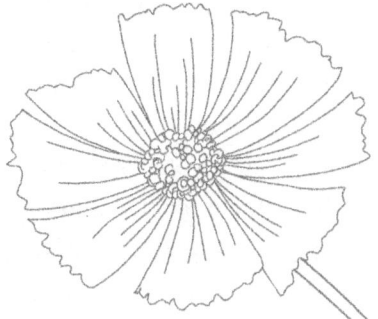

The Train

"It is said that your life flashes before your eyes just before you die. That is true, it's called Life."

—TERRY PRATCHETT

THREE MONTHS AFTER MY DIVORCE, I MET CHRIS ALLEN. He was a consultant at the company that I worked with. We were both new to the company. Chris was six foot tall, with dirty-blonde hair and the bluest eyes I had ever seen. I also *noticed* that he had wide shoulders and toned arms. I knew him but did not know him well. However, he seemed very needy all the time. He would come to my desk about three times a day asking for help. Chris did this for months, and eventually, he mustered up his courage to strike up a conversation with me.

It was refreshing that Chris wanted to know everything about me. He even offered to go to the park or movies with me if I were interested. I thought to myself, "What a nice guy." Little did I know he was gauging my interest, but since I never really dated anyone or even went on a real date, I had no idea what flirting or courting looked like.

Finally, after three long months, my friend Veronica informed me that Chris was very interested in me. I told her that I liked him too. He was a nice person.

She laughed. "You are very naïve, Sally. Chris *likes* you, and he is gauging your interest."

I looked at her, baffled. "What do you mean?" I asked.

She laughed again. "He wants to go on a date with you."

We looked at each other and burst out laughing. It was the first time in years I had a bellyaching laugh. We laughed so hard that a few people came out of their offices to see what was going on. Finally, after we wiped our eyes and composed ourselves, I asked her what I should do.

"Clearly, you have two choices," she said. "Tell him you are not interested in going to the movie or park with him next time he mentions it, or tell him you will go with him."

"It cannot be that simple. What if he turns out to be a serial killer?" I asked.

"You need to stop reading Stephen King and Dean Koonz books," she retorted.

We fell into another fit of giggles. I thought about it for a second. It would be nice to try out this dating thing. I shivered at the thought. The thought of dating was scarier than I ever

7 • The Train

imagined. I gave it another few weeks before I mustered up the courage and made a decision. After all, Chris seemed like a nice guy; he was not rude and rash but rather polite. I decided that it was a good thing that he gauged my interest first.

A few weeks later, Chris was thanking me for sending out a fax when I surprised him by saying he could thank me by taking me to the movies. I pretended to be typing away at my computer as I spoke to him. I never once looked at him. I got flustered after realizing how stupid that sounded, and I quickly backpedaled.

"Well, I mean, you don't have to thank me that way. Verbal thank you is okay."

I finally had the courage to look at him. What I saw floored me. He was beet red and speechless. Well, so was I. We both stared at each other, unable to speak. Finally, he gave me an affirmative nod and walked away. Not even a second after he left, Veronica ran over to my desk, looking at me in anticipation.

"Well?" She blurted. "Are you going to tell me what just happened?"

After I told her, we both ran to the bathroom and giggled so hard that I thought I would pee myself.

Chris and I went on our first date that weekend. Our first movie was *Saving Private Ryan*. I fell asleep halfway through the film.

Visitation with Richard and Jay became regular and routine. It would seem like all was going well. Jay was finally accepting the divorce and leaving me alone, or so I thought. A few months into dating Chris, Jay was dropping off Richard when all hell broke loose. Our pick-up location was at the train station.

As soon as they got off the train, I knew that something was wrong. Richard was pale and looked terrified. Jay looked like he had been drinking all weekend without any sleep, a look that I was all-too-familiar with.

My blood ran cold; something was very wrong. All the hair stood up at the back of my neck. As Jay walked menacingly towards me, I called Richard to come over to me. I did not realize that my voice was trembling. Richard started crying as he broke loose from Jay and ran over to me, hugging my waist tightly. My heart broke as his soft crying turned into sobbing.

Richard was repeating, "I am sorry, Mommy. I am sorry, Mommy."

"Oh crap," I thought as Jay walked over to me and shouted, "Who is Chris?"

What did Chris have to do with anything? I thought, and then it hit me. Jay must have been drilling Richard for information about me. Richard had just met Chris the Friday before his visitation. Jay knew about Chris!

"Chris is a friend," I stuttered.

"A friend. Is that the friend you left me for?" Jay screamed.

I looked him straight in the eye and said, "It is none of your business. We are no longer married."

That was a big mistake. Even as the words came out of my mouth, I knew that I had just put myself and perhaps Richard's life in danger. Jay lunged at me and grabbed me around the throat. His eyes were glassy, and his breath reeked of alcohol. His clothes were wrinkled, and I could smell the sour odor of sweat mingled with alcohol oozing from his pores. I

7 • The Train

gagged and started to struggle, but he squeezed harder, all the while shouting, "You lying b***h!"

Jay dragged me over to a pillar, held me up against it, and with one hand on my throat, started slapping me with the other.

He repeatedly shouted, "Who is Chris? Why are you seeing him? You are still my wife."

Jay was still in denial that we were divorced. In his mind, that piece of paper meant nothing. In the background, I could hear people screaming at him to let me go. I felt light-headed as someone came over to Jay and tried to shove him off me. Jay turned around and pushed the guy away, screaming that this was a quarrel between a wife and a husband.

"You said you won't hurt my mommy!" Richard was now screaming, but he had no effect because Jay kept choking me. With hands still on my throat, Jay dragged me over to the edge of the train platform. By now, I was dizzy. My legs were wobbly. I tried to pull away from him, but he stood behind me and grabbed my tiny, one-hundred-pound body close to his, his arms tightly around my waist. I had no idea what he was doing until I saw the train headlights at the end of the tunnel. This is not the light you want to see at the end of the tunnel when your furious drunk ex-husband is holding you at the edge of the train platform. Oh my God, I thought, Jay is going to throw us onto the train tracks in front of Richard, and I was helpless to do anything.

Jay held me tighter and whispered, "If I cannot have you, no one else can."

I stopped struggling for fear of falling onto the tracks and stood stiffly in his arms. I saw my life flash before my eyes and wondered if this was the end for me. I snapped out of my thoughts as Jay pushed me right up to the edge of the platform. "Why is no one coming to my rescue?" I thought. Then I realized that it must have looked like Jay and I had made up and were hugging and waiting for the train.

Richard was standing right beside us. He had stopped crying. He looked at me wide-eyed as I glanced down at him. No words would come out. I started praying for Richard as the train got closer. Lord, protect my boy from this madman.

I must have passed out because the next thing I knew, I woke up lying on the train platform, and two people were kneeling beside me, asking if I was okay. I looked around. Richard was sitting by my side, looking stunned.

To this day, I do not know what possessed Jay to do what he did in front of Richard. Nor do I understand why I was not splattered onto the train tracks. I have stopped trying to figure it out and just count my blessings. I wondered what would have happened if I fought back. I cringed because I have never felt so ashamed and helpless, mainly because I could not help my son.

My entire body was hurting as I struggled up from the platform. I thanked the folks around me, hopped on the next train, and went straight to the police station. I filed a police report, and two days later, Jay was arrested. He spent a few days in jail. I stopped visitations and told him that he had to take me to court if he wanted to see Richard. Jay never responded or tried to see Richard again until six years later when Chris tried to adopt Richard.

After being served with adoption documents, Jay came after us full force with an attorney, claiming that I kidnapped

7 • The Train

Richard and he could not find Richard for six years. He also claimed that Richard did not want to be adopted and was being coerced. Little did he know, the adoption request was Richard's idea. The adoption proceeding took only a few hours as the judge saw right through Jay, kicked him out of the courtroom, and allowed Chris to adopt Richard.

PRESENT MOMENT

Perhaps you're wondering why I would even want to date again, let alone get married again. Yes, Chris and I eventually got married. People are jaded all the time because of horrible relationships. I refused to live in fear. Living in fear meant that Jay still had a stronghold and power over me. I was determined to take back my power by living a life without dread and anxiety. I chose to live a life of resiliency and boldness.

This means that I charged forward in bravery, regardless of what challenges I faced. If I can, you can too. I have said over and over again that we always have a choice. I hate the saying, "It is what it is." It is such a cop-out answer, and it is not true. We always have a choice. What will you choose? Will you be held hostage by your past or by a current situation, or will you overcome your obstacles and step out into your bold, brave, and beautiful self? It is only when we choose the latter that we can live a life of resiliency.

Finally, life is too short to live in fear and regret. How far will you go to live a life of resiliency and fearlessness? You have the choice to be intentional, to take action now.

My son Richard learned how to be intentional in his decisions and has learned how to live a life of resiliency. He is following his dreams. Today, with his blessings, I am writing this book. As for Jay, sadly, he died two years ago. God bless his soul. I truly hope that he can rest in peace.

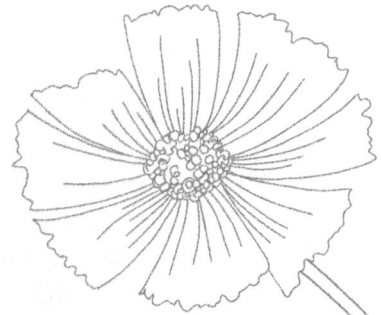

8

Take Back Your Power

*"I can be changed by what happens to me,
but I refuse to be reduced by it."*

—MAYA ANGELOU

By now, you have seen that my life has not been a bed of roses. I have weaved in and out of challenges throughout my forty-eight years on this earth, and 2020 was no different. It was a year that was challenging for all of us. Every one of us was impacted in some way by the pandemic.

Chris and I were affected in many ways, but the two most devastating events were the death of my friend, Annie, and having to quit my job. Because of COVID-19, I could not travel to my friend's funeral and could not say goodbye to her in the way that I wanted. That was devastating and took a toll on me, but I finally reconciled and had a Zoom memorial with our friends in New York.

I thought that was the worst of 2020 until something devastating happened at work, and I decided to quit my job. I have learned, once again, that in the blink of an eye, my entire life can change. I take nothing for granted. While both events were tumultuous, I knew that I had to be resilient and draw from all that I had learned over the past years. I was faced with the choices I discussed in the last chapter. I could choose to be intentional and take action, or I could crash like a pile of rubble.

Up until 2020, I never stopped to think about what the driving force behind my life was for the past twenty-two years after I ran away from Jay. I did not realize that I was living a life of resiliency. I kept going and never stopped to assess what drove me to live a resilient life until I was asked to speak at a like-minded lunch.

My friend and coach, Missy, asked me to speak about how 2020 has impacted me and how I was able to stay resilient. The more I thought about the word resilient, the more I started digging into my past and current life to see how this word has shaped me. Working at the bank came to mind, and what I found was both startling and eye-opening.

That was twenty-five years ago. I was only twenty-four years old. I had just arrived two years prior from my native country before taking that job. We spoke English in Guyana, but it was very broken English. That alone, compounded with my daily abuse at home, made me very timid at work. Management was awful at the bank, and therefore the culture was terrible. People were disrespecting each other and without consequences.

Being the new girl and not understanding the American culture or what company culture should look like, I was brutally taken advantage of. I had to stay late every night and close the bank. I was called a piece of crap and racially discriminated against daily. I was sick to my stomach.

It took every ounce of my energy to get out of bed daily to go to work. However, I endured all of it for three years because I did not know that I could do better. Not once did it cross my mind that what was happening was not normal and that no human being should be treated like that.

Being stuck in the bondage of fear—mine or others—is paralyzing and debilitating, but I grew up thinking that was how life was. I did not know that I could be the person I am today. I did not realize that I could feel differently and think differently. For a long time, I allowed my circumstances to define me and the choices I made. I allowed people to dictate my life and control me.

When I realized there was more to life than just my miserable existence, and when I vowed to stand up for others, there was a paradigm shift. A seed was planted, and resiliency was born. I was not aware that I was nurturing that seed until I mustered up my courage to leave Jay. That little seed continued to grow, and now it has blossomed into a beautiful flower that continues on because it is fed with my core power: resilience.

The word *resilience* is the foundation of my book.

Twenty-five years ago, I lacked the resilience to navigate basic situations in life. I realized that I lacked the very things that I utilize *now* to help me live a life of strength, stability, and resilience.

I have grown quite a bit since the bank job. It only took me three months—not three years like it did at the bank—to make a decision when I was faced with the choice to stay at my job and be resentful or leave and take my power back. I chose to take my power back and left with my head held high and my pride intact. I dug deep into why I was able to act so quickly. How was I able to make that decision so swiftly, especially in the middle of a pandemic?

I realized that my "why" was the word *resilience*.

Now don't think for a minute that the decision to leave my job was made in a day. You see, I was comfortable at this job for ten years. I loved this company and poured everything I had into it. I worked hard to achieve where I was. I put in many extra hours. I had many great friends. The decision to leave was not easy.

A week later, a friend asked me what gave me the strength to leave a well-paying job in the middle of a pandemic. I told her, "Everything I lacked twenty-five years ago." When I made that one decision to leave my abusive husband, I started to build within me the principles that I now live by. They are:

Do Something Meaningful Daily & Stay Hopeful: I laughed out loud when this realization came to me. Do something meaningful with my life, and make every day hopeful. Twenty-five years ago, I was so empty emotionally that I had nothing to give to anyone. How could I make my day meaningful when I was living in a vacuum of hopelessness?

Today, everyone I meet and the actions that I take have meaning and are hopeful. I love my life and cherish every moment. I realize that life is but fleeting, and I am thankful that I get to wake up daily and enjoy life. I make it meaningful also by learning one new thing each day and making someone smile each day. No matter what I am going through. I know that there is light at the end of the tunnel. God does not give us more than we can handle.

Personal Values: Personal values are the foundation and guiding principles used for the daily decisions that we make. They are our moral compass. They help us make decisions and navigate through life. They are unshakable and unbreakable. When I was young and allowed others to make decisions for me, I did not understand personal values and how they applied to everyday life. I had no foundation on how to live my life at the time. I did not realize how fundamental these values would become to me and how they would change my life.

My values are courage and faith. Every decision that I make is based on these two words. How did I apply them to the 2020 job situation? I was courageous and quit because I had faith that I would land on my feet again. I had faith that my experiences and connections that I built over the years would come through. My faith is based on a *big* God. He has never failed me. Over the years, I have held on to this scripture that has delivered me from fear repeatedly: "Have I not commanded you? Be strong and courageous. Do not be afraid; do not be discouraged, for the Lord your God will be with you wherever you go" (Joshua 1:9 NIV).

Life Experiences: I was curious and typed "life experiences" in Google to see what would pop up. Per Merriam Webster Dictionary: life experiences mean "experience and knowledge gained through living" The part that really stuck with me is "gain through living" You see, twenty-five years ago, I had no positive life experiences to draw from. I was frequently consumed by waves of fear, insecurity, and despair that crashed down on me every time I tried to rise up. My positive emotional bank account was empty. I was not living, I was existing.

Today, I have had so many good experiences from the past twenty years that I was able to draw from those experiences to make a decision quickly. Reflecting on my past guided me through this current situation. I can keep my power or give it away. I chose to keep it. Whatever challenges you are going through, I hope you choose to keep your power as well.

Proactivity: Now that you have made it this far reading my book, can you see me being proactive twenty-five years ago? (On a side note, my heart swells up as I write this. I love that you got a glimpse of my life, and I hope that it's helping you as you are reading. Even if you just take away one thing, that makes it worth the two years that I labored over this book!) When there is no hope, it is easy to quit. Remember how many times I considered jumping in front of a train? You cannot be proactive when there is no will to live. You cannot be proactive when you are just surviving and not thriving.

I could have easily swept my 2020 job situation under the rug and not deal with it—because I was working from home, like everyone else, when the pandemic hit—but I knew I had to take action. I figured out what needed to be done, formulated a plan, and executed my plan. When you finally harness that power to fight for yourself and stand up for what is right, it forces you to be proactive. Where there is a will, there is a way.

Connections: We were made for relationships and connecting with people. It's the experience of oneness. God did not create us to be isolated. It is why so many of us suffered during this 2020 pandemic. I was forbidden to make any kind of human connection when I arrived in America; it was not a command that was hard for me to obey. I did not trust people anyway. Everyone who was supposed to love me, take care of me, and keep me safe had failed me repeatedly. I never had a safe place or a safe person to turn to. I was always battling my demons alone.

Building strong, positive relationships with loved ones and friends provided me with the much-needed support and acceptance in good and bad times. Remember, I started building my network while I worked at the bank. I never stopped once I started. I have so many great friends. They are the people who would call me on my bullshit, and they are also the shoulders that I will cry on. Those shoulders have seen and experienced many ugly, snot-dripping tears.

After I threw a fit over quitting my job in 2020, I did the next best thing after I dramatized for a few weeks. I called up my tribe and shared with them. I am thankful that my tribe is not a "yes" tribe. I know for a fact that if I were being a drama queen, they would have told me to "knock it off" and get back to work. But every one of them felt the same way as I did, and they supported my decision.

Paying It Forward: I love volunteering. It gives me a sense of accomplishment and purpose every day. Even before I quit my job, I started volunteering more. It was in the middle of the pandemic, and the need was great. Because I was so focused on other people, I had no time for a poor-me pity party. I stayed hopeful and useful. I can't change the past, but I can always look toward the future.

Self-Care: Self-care means knowing your limits and having the self-awareness that you need to slow down and take care of yourself. In a nutshell, it means knowing who you are, what sets you off, what replenishes you, and what drains you. This may seem basic to you, but you will be amazed by how many of us do not know when we need self-care and how to take care of ourselves.

Pausing for reflection is so crucial to self-care. It helps us assess where we are mentally. I do my best to pause and reflect when I am exercising, hiking, or biking. I also get plenty of sleep. I practice stress management and relaxation techniques, such as yoga, meditation, deep breathing, and prayer. Ah, and yes, I do get my hair and nails done frequently, and I love a good massage.

The Resilience Process

While I have used all the techniques above to help build resiliency, I have also used some processes that continually help my coaching clients and me move forward in life and face inevitable challenges. I would like to share with you as we close:

Here is the process that I use when making a change or decision. This is how I applied it to the decision to leave my job:

1. Understand what is holding you back. I did not make a snap decision to leave in a hot minute. I knew *something* was holding me back. I had to take a self-assessment and figure it out. I realized that it was my fear of losing my income and my health insurance. It was also fear that no one was going to hire me in the middle of a pandemic. Those were valid concerns. I had to assess my finances to overcome these fears.

2. Develop a plan for *if* and *when* you fail. Mine was accountability. I knew that if I did not share my plan with others, I would chicken out. I shared it in detail with my friends, family, and coach and asked them to hold me accountable.
3. Put a system in place. If we do not have a system in place, we will fail. It is not about any single accomplishment. It is about the cycle of continuous improvement. So, I quit my job. What now? What is my plan? What is my system? I started reaching out to my network. I updated my resume and my LinkedIn profile. I scheduled weekly job searches, not randomly, but deliberate blocks of hours when I would sit at my computer and search for jobs. Most importantly, I put in place the means to finish this book. I needed to change my behavior and my daily pattern. I needed to be intentional.

I was able to leave in three months because I am a different person from the girl I was twenty years ago. Now I can be identified as someone with personal values, someone hopeful and optimistic, someone proactive and strong—and most importantly, I do not take crap from anyone.

People say that I am brave. I am not. I am terrified half of the time. I just do brave things despite my fears; all people see are the end results. They do not see the struggle in between. You see, writing this book was scary, I knew that I risked losing part of my family. There were nights when I was jolted awake with fears and anxiety about putting my life out there, wondering what impact it could have, but I pushed forward in bravery because I know in my heart that *someone* out there needs to hear my story!

To quote Brené Brown: "One day you will tell your story of how you've overcome what you are going through now, and it will become part of someone else's survival guide."

This is my hope for you—that my story becomes your survival guide. Together we can move forward and create a far brighter, more hopeful, and much stronger future.

Acknowledgments

It is by the grace of God that I have completed this book. I knew that God kept me alive for such a time as this, but I could not have done it without my two publishing experts, Patricia Ross and Ronda Taylor. Thank you so much for working with me tirelessly and endlessly and for kicking my butt whenever I was ready to throw in the towel.

Thank you to my friends, Ruth and Janice, who are always there for me. "Jersey girls" forever!

I want to express my deep and sincere gratitude to my Rooted Bible Study girls and my sister, Naz. I could not have done this without your daily prayers, encouragement, and support.

Thank you to my friend and coach, Missy Day, who encouraged me to write my story and constantly reaffirm how powerful my story is.

Finally, I am eternally grateful to my husband, son, and in-laws for their never-ending love and support.

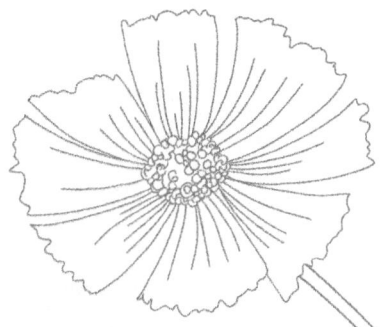

About the Author

Sally Allen was born in Guyana, South America, and she immigrated to the United States in 1993. She began writing her debut non-fiction after she started believing that her story was not "normal," and that she could help others by telling it.

She has been an outspoken advocate for women and fights against child sex trafficking locally and globally.

She currently lives in Nevada with her husband and three dogs. She is also a mom to an adult son. When she is not volunteering, she spends most of her time traveling, reading, cooking, biking, and hiking.

Ready to make a change and live a resilient life?

*Keep in touch with me.
Follow my blog:
sallyallencoaching.com/blog
I would love to hear your story.*

Connect with me at:
Website: sallyallencoaching.com
Facebook: @sallyallencoaching
Instagram: @sallyallen_828

www.ingramcontent.com/pod-product-compliance
Lightning Source LLC
LaVergne TN
LVHW041340080426
835512LV00006B/552